W9-ARF-105

Amazing Aaron to Zero Zippers

An Introduction to Baseball History

Roger Maris takes away a home run in spectacular fashion.

Amazing Aaron to Zero Zippers

An Introduction to Baseball History

by

Matt Nadel

Foreword by

Jim Palmer

SUMMER
GAME
BOOKS

copyright © 2014 by Matt Nadel

Published by Summer Game Books
All rights reserved.

No part of this publication may be reproduced, stored in a retrieval system, or transmitted in any form by any process – electronic, mechanical, photocopying, recording, or otherwise – without prior written permission from the copyright owner and the publisher. The scanning, uploading, and distribution of this book via the internet or any other means without the permission of the publisher is illegal.

ISBN: 978-1-938545-46-7 (pbk)
ISBN: 978-1-938545-47-4 (ebook)

For information about permissions, bulk purchases, or additional distribution, write to Summer Game Books
P. O. Box 818
South Orange, NJ 07079
or contact the publisher at
www.summergamebooks.com

Photo Credits:
The following pictures have been licensed from the AP: All images front cover; interior photos of Jackie Robinson (p15), Carlton Fisk (p69), Joe Carter (p71), Bill Mazeroski (p72), Willie Mays (p76).
All other pictures, with the exception of those on p75 and p93, are licensed from the National Baseball Hall of Fame Library, Cooperstown, N.Y.

All author proceeds will be donated to four of Matt's favorite baseball charities: The Jackie Robinson Foundation, The National Baseball Hall of Fame and Museum, Turn 2 Foundation and The ALS Association.

Dedication

I dedicate this book to every person who has ever enjoyed the game of baseball, whether as a player, a coach or a fan.

Table of Contents

Acknowledgments

There have been many people who have helped me along my journey in one way or another, and I'd like to take this moment to thank them for what they've done for me. In no particular order, thank you to:

- Fred Lynn, my first MLB player interview, who granted an unknown baseball blogger an interview in 2012, and who has been encouraging ever since.
- Jeff Idelson, the President of the National Baseball Hall of Fame and Museum, for getting me involved in many Hall of Fame events and for always supporting my passion. Also, thank you's to my other friends at the Hall including Brad Horn, Craig Muder, Roger Lansing, Donny Lowe, Dan Wallis and John Horne.
- John Thorn, MLB's official historian, who, when I was only 13 years old, appointed me as a Pro Blogger on MLB.com.
- Mark Newman at MLBlogs, who has always spread the word about my baseball history blog.
- Greg Amsinger, MLB Network anchor, who made my dreams come true by having me appear on MLB Hot Stove. Thanks also to Harold Reynolds and, of course, Gina Hemphill, the person behind the scenes who makes it all happen.
- Bud Selig, the former Commissioner of MLB, and Rob Manfred, the Commissioner, who both granted me great interviews and supported my work.
- Billy Crystal, who through his humor during our interview taught me that history can be a lot of fun.
- Andy Abrams, probably my biggest fan who isn't a family member, who created my blog catchphrase "all the buzz on what wuzz."
- Marty Appel, author of one my all-time favorite books, *Pinstripe Empire*, for showing me nothing but kindness all the time.

- Mark Attanasio, the owner of the Milwaukee Brewers, who was super-friendly to me during our first interview and who has continued to support my work.
- President George W. Bush, the first (and so far only) President I've ever interviewed, who showed me that I have to keep doing this.
- Lou Oppenheim, CEO of Headline Media Management, who always has time for me and consistently provides an encouraging word.
- Spencer Baretz, head of Hellerman Baretz Communications, along with Jason Milch, Brian Pitts and Molly McLeod, who have done so much for me.
- Casey Close, baseball division head at Excel Sports, for always cheering on my work, even during his most hectic times of the year.
- Josh Flagner, of *More Than a Fan*, the first person to ever invite me to guest write on a site that wasn't my own.
- Joe Nardini and Matt Orso of *New Jersey Baseball Magazine*, who created a special section for me on their site and gave me my first paycheck ever.
- Reynaldo Cruz of *Universo Beisbol*, my amigo from Cuba, who allowed me to reconnect to my Spanish heritage and to spread the baseball history gospel in Latin America.
- Mike Lynch, the man behind *Seamheads*, who by inviting me to guest blog on his site has validated what I do.
- Thomas Murphy and Robyn Vandenberg of *Hump Day w/ Murph and That Sports Chick*, who have helped me build my confidence tremendously.
- Steve Serby of the *New York Post* who has encouraged me from the very first day we ever met in New Jersey.
- Ken Davidoff, *New York Post* Yankees beat writer, who has given me some sage advice over the past two years.
- Nick Dennison, the first fan to ever recognize me in public.
- All of the people in my dad's office at Seward & Kissel LLP, and my dad's friends, who have shown me so many acts of kindness, including John Tavss, Jack Rigney, Jim Abbott, Rob Van Grover, Dale Christensen, Royce Akiva, Julia Graham, Danielle Rettinger, Howard Altman, Nathan Romano, Jeremy Siegel, Gerald Polizzi and Jason Duffy.

Special thanks to the author of the book's foreword, Jim Palmer, the first Hall of Famer I ever interviewed and the first former MLB player that I actually ever spoke with. He's been a class act from the very first time we spoke. He's treated me like a baseball journalist from day one, not just some kid. He's a real gentleman. And the same goes for Jim's manager, Ric Bachrach, who has been supportive of me in countless ways.

Special thanks to my cover designer and long-time family friend, Carol Moskot of Carol Moskot Design + Direction, for designing a great cover. It rocks, Carol!

Special thanks also to my publisher at Summer Game Books, Walter Friedman, who believed in my vision for this book, and who has given me the best advice that a first-time author could ever hope to get.

Last, but not least, I would like to thank my extended family for constantly applauding my work, my mom and sister for all of their support, and probably my biggest helper, my dad, without whom I couldn't have lasted this long in the blogging world.

Foreword
by Jim Palmer

Having been involved with baseball now for about 60 years, I can tell you that what I've learned about this great game and its history has helped shape the man that I've become today. Starting out with my days as a kid pitching in Little League and dreaming that maybe one day I could be the next Cy Young, through my Baltimore Orioles years, to my induction into the Baseball Hall of Fame, and now my current job as a baseball broadcaster, the constant for me has been the game. Baseball is a beautiful game with a rich history dating back to the 1860's. While the world has certainly changed significantly in the last 150 or so years, baseball has pretty much remained the same.

You may ask, "well if baseball is virtually unchanged for so long, isn't it completely out of date?" The answer is a resounding "No!" Where else but baseball can you have over a century of drama, comedy, strategy, second guessing, triumph, tragedy, heroes, villains, inspiration, loyalty, rivalries, family outings, grand pavilions of battle, nicknames galore, unbelievable endings, more statistics than you could ever imagine, not to mention hot dogs, peanuts and Cracker Jacks?? All this history is sewn into baseball's fabric, an area that has inspired thousands of books over the years.

So then, why do we need yet another baseball history book? What's so special about this one? A lot! Matt Nadel isn't your typical baseball historian by any stretch of the imagination. Matt is just 15 years old and started blogging about baseball history in April 2012 under the *Baseball with Matt* blog name. He started his blog because he was finding that many kids and even adults knew very little about baseball history, and he wanted to remedy that. Eventually, Matt was discovered by John Thorn, Major League Baseball's official historian, and John appointed Matt as a Pro Blogger on MLB.com. Since then, Matt has written many great posts and has also interviewed numerous Hall of Famers, as well as President George W. Bush, Billy Crystal, MLB Commissioner Bud Selig, Hall of Fame President Jeff Idelson and many others. He has acted as the youth reporter at the Baseball Hall of Fame Classic, and has even appeared live on the MLB Network. Through it all, Matt's infectious, youthful enthusiasm for the game comes through in each blog post that he writes, each video that he posts on his YouTube channel, and now in each chapter of this book.

All I can say is READ THIS BOOK!! Matt has poured the essential points of 150 years of baseball history into it in a way that only a kid could do. While this book will teach you a lot, I think what it may do even better is inspire you to read even more about the game that I love so much.

Introduction
by Matt Nadel

Have you ever heard of the "Shot Heard Round the World?" Do you know who the Human Vacuum Cleaner or the Man of Steal was? Do you know what a Triple Crown is? While these may sound like famous battles or comic book characters or horse races, they all have one thing in common... the history of baseball.

This book will take you on an alphabetical adventure through the history of America's national pastime, baseball. You will learn about the most important who's, what's, when's, where's and why's, including the best players, the most iconic parks and teams, and the greatest moments.

Whether you're a kid just learning about the game, or an adult who needs a baseball history refresher, this book will give you a real understanding of baseball history through my eyes, MLB.com's youngest baseball history Pro Blogger, Matt Nadel, of *Baseball with Matt*.

As a seven-year-old boy, I never really liked reading fiction books, but I was immediately drawn to the long history of baseball, dating back to the 1800's, so I started reading baseball biographies. Because of this, baseball history has always been one of my favorite things to research, talk about, and write about. By the time I was 13, I was pretty knowledgeable about the history of our national pastime, and I realized that most of my friends knew nothing about it. Without that knowledge, I felt that they lacked the proper historical perspective to truly enjoy baseball today. So, in April 2012 I started my blog, *Baseball with Matt,* to help teach kids and adults about baseball history. *Baseball with Matt,* and now this book, are ways that I hope to share why baseball is such a great sport and why I have devoted the last two and a half years of my life to it. I hope that after reading this book, you will love and appreciate the game as much as I do.

People often tell me that they don't like history. All I can say to that is don't ever forget that what is happening today is tomorrow's history!!

If you'd like to read some of my prior work, please check out my blog, *Baseball with Matt* on either *www.baseballwithmatt.blogspot.com* or *www.baseballwithmatt.mlblogs.com.* I also guest write on various other sites like *Seamheads, More Than a Fan, Universo Beisbol, NJ Baseball Magazine, Baseball Essential, Sqor* and *the Patch.*

If you'd like to follow me on Twitter, please go to **@baseballwmatt**. If you'd like to check out my YouTube channel, please go to YouTube and type in Matt Nadel. If you'd like to write me, please send an email to **mattamdad@gmail.com**.

And now, as I always say in my blog, it's time for "all the buzz on what wuzz."

Baseball History Resources

While it is impossible to come up with a complete list of every baseball website and book covering baseball history, here are some that I have found to be very useful and informative when writing my blog, *Baseball with Matt.*

Websites:

- Baseball Almanac (*http://baseball-almanac.com*)
- Baseball Hall of Fame and Museum (*http://baseballhall.org*)
- Baseball Past and Present (*http://baseballpastandpresent.com*)
- Baseball Reference (*http://baseball-reference.com*)
- Baseball Reflections (*http://baseballreflections.com*)
- Dugout Legends (*http://dugoutlegends.com*)
- MLB (*http://mlb.mlb.com/home*)
- National Pastime (*http://nationalpastime.com*)
- Negro Leagues Baseball Museum (*http://nlbm.com*)
- Seamheads (*http://seamheads.com*)
- This Great Game (*http://thisgreatgame.com*)

Books:

- Baseball's Golden Age: The Photographs of Charles Conlon (*Neal McCabe, ed.*)
- The Baseball Maniac's Almanac (*Bert Randolph Sugar*)
- Baseball's Unforgettables (*Mac Davis*)
- The Era (*Roger Kahn*)
- First Pitch (*John Thorn*)
- Glory in the Fall: The Greatest Moments in World Series History (*Peter Golenbock*)
- The Glory of Their Times (*Lawrence Ritter*)

- Greats of the Game (*Ray Robinson and Christopher Jennison*)
- The 100 Greatest Baseball Players of All Time (*Lawrence Ritter and Donald Honig*)
- 100 Years of the World Series (*Eric Enders*)
- Pinstripe Empire (*Marty Appel*)
- Total Baseball: The Official Encyclopedia of Major League Baseball (*John Thorn, Pete Palmer, Michael Gershman*)
- Treasures of the Baseball Hall of Fame (*John Thorn*)

Amazing Aaron

Henry "Hank" Aaron

There are good baseball players, great ones, and just plain legendary ones. Henry "Hank" Aaron indisputably falls into the category of legendary player. His contributions to baseball have made the game what it has become today and he is definitely one of the very greatest players of all time.

Hank Aaron was born in a section of Mobile, Alabama called "Down the Bay" on February 5, 1934 and spent much of his early life in quiet Toulminville, Alabama. Despite the isolated rural setting, Aaron was not sheltered from intense bigotry directed at African-Americans back then in the South. Because Major League Baseball did not allow black players until Jackie Robinson came along in 1947 (for more on Jackie Robinson, check out "Revolutionary Robinson"), Hank's first professional baseball experience was in the Negro Leagues in 1951, playing for the Indianapolis Clowns. He was later signed by the major league Boston Braves in June of 1952, because of his great play in Indianapolis. After

A young Henry Aaron.

two years in the minor leagues, Hank was brought up to the majors for the start of the 1954 season and joined the Braves, who had moved as a team to Milwaukee, Wisconsin in 1953.

Hammerin' Hank hits number 715.

On April 13, 1954, Hammerin' Hank made his major league debut and was hitless in five at bats against Cincinnati. Two days later, he got his first major league hit, a double against the Cardinals, and he hit his first major league home run on April 23. Aaron batted .280 for the year with thirteen homers before he broke his ankle on September 5th.

In 1955, Hank became an All Star for the first time in his career. He would go on to make a record 25 All Star game appearances!! He hit .314 that year with 27 home runs.

In 1957, Aaron won his only MVP Award, batting .322, also finishing first in the league in homers and runs batted in. He led the Braves to the World Series against the Yankees, which the Braves won in seven games (for more about the World Series, check out "Wonderful World Series"). He then took them back to the Series the next year, but the Yanks got their revenge.

Over the next few years, Aaron had some of his best games and some of the best seasons of any major league player. On June 21, 1959, he hit three home runs in a game against the Giants (his only three home run game).

Aaron almost won the Triple Crown in 1963 by leading the league with 44 homers and 130 RBI, but he finished third in batting average at .319, seven points behind the leader Tommy Davis (for more about Triple Crowns, check out "Triumphant Trifectas").

The Braves moved from Milwaukee to Atlanta, Georgia in 1966, which was very sad for Hank, because he really loved the Wisconsin fans and they loved him. Nonetheless, he still achieved some major career milestones after the move, including getting his 3,000th hit and hitting his 500th and 600th home runs. With every home run, Hank inched his way closer to Babe Ruth's career home run record of 714.

Finally, at the start of his 21st season, on April 8, 1974, against pitcher Al Downing of the Los Angeles Dodgers, despite all of the racial harassment he had to endure throughout his homer chase, Hank sent a shot over the left field fence for his record-breaking 715th career homer to become MLB's home run king!!!! The baseball world went wild with excitement!

Aaron finished his career with some amazing statistics: 3,771 hits, third all time, along with major league baseball records of 755 homers (which has since been broken by Barry Bonds with 762) and 2,297 RBI. Aaron's career was magnificent and should be remembered forever, because it was one of the best of all time.

Always Able

Henry Aaron ended the 1973 season one short of Babe Ruth's career home run mark. With the world watching, Aaron wasted no time finishing his assault on the record, tying it on Opening Day on his first swing of the season!

After a day off and an 0-for-2, the Braves traveled to Atlanta for their home opener, where Aaron very much wanted to break the record. After walking in the first inning, Aaron's first swing of the game again resulted in a home run, this time number 715!

Booming Babe

Babe Ruth

The Babe while still on the Red Sox.

There is an ongoing argument over who is the greatest pure hitter in baseball history. Some say it was Stan Musial who played for the St. Louis Cardinals, or Boston Red Sox legend Ted Williams, or even Hank Aaron. I believe that in order to earn the title of the "Greatest Hitter Ever," the player needs to be iconic, revolutionary, and put up incredible numbers. No one who has played Major League Baseball embodied those characteristics better as a hitter than the one and only moon-shape-faced Babe Ruth.

George Herman "Babe" Ruth was born in Baltimore, Maryland on February 6, 1895. His home life was a difficult one, so he spent his childhood at St. Mary's Industrial School for Boys. There, he discovered his love for baseball. One of the monks at the school, Brother Matthias, helped Ruth with his baseball skills, and also served as a fatherly figure to the young Babe. When Babe first started playing ball, he was a catcher, but he was asked to join the minor league Baltimore Orioles as a pitcher in 1914. Soon, his contract was purchased by the Boston Red Sox. When he first got to the majors, Babe was one of the best pitchers in the American League. He actually had a 94-46 record with a 2.28 ERA in his career, (including 5-0 during his years with the Yankees, even though he was a full-time hitter with them). Babe often said that the record he was most proud of was one that involves pitching, namely when he threw 29.2 consecutive shutout innings during World Series play (a record later broken by another Yankee, Whitey Ford).

As the Babe was mowing them down as a pitcher, World War I suddenly interfered, forcing many ballplayers across the major leagues to hang up their cleats and serve their country in war. Despite Ruth's excellence on the mound, his hitting was so good the Red Sox wanted to get his bat in the lineup more often, and they asked him to focus more on playing the outfield and batting than on pitching. Ruth did just that and, in 1919, Ruth hit 29 homers to set a single-season home run record, along with a league-leading 113 runs batted in, while still pitching 133.1 innings and compiling a 9-5 record. However, for various reasons, the most important of which was a need for money, Red Sox owner Harry Frazee sold the "Bambino" (one of the Babe's many nicknames) to the Yankees before the 1920 season. From then until 2004, the Red Sox didn't win any Fall Classics (another term used for the World Series), creating the legendary "Curse of the Bambino." And it was with the Yankees that the Babe's legend really took flight.

Ruth smacked a massive 54 homers in 1920 for the Yanks. That total was more than all but two entire teams in MLB!! In 1921 and 1922, the "Sultan of Swat" (another great nickname for The Babe) continued to dominate like no one had ever done before, as he helped the Yankees make their first two World Series appearances. Sadly for Ruth, they lost both of those Series to the New York Giants, but come 1923, the Yanks changed ballparks and with it, their luck, too. Because of Ruth's popularity, the team was able to move from the Polo Grounds, which they had shared with the Giants (before that they had played at Hilltop Park), into Yankee Stadium in the Bronx. That is why it became known as "the house that Ruth built," and also why the Yankees are often now called the "Bronx Bombers."

The Babe always took care of his fans.

On Opening Day of the new stadium, Ruth hit the first homer ever, helping the Yankees defeat his former team, the Red Sox, 4-1. When the regular season ended, Babe had hit 41 homers and batted a career high .393. This was the only year that the Babe won an MVP award,

The Sultan of Swat smashes another homer.

because back then, once you won an MVP award, you were not eligible to win any more. Also, the Yankees won the pennant and their first ever World Series title (against the Giants, four games to two).

The Yanks reached the World Series again in 1926, this time versus the Cardinals. In the bottom of the ninth inning of Game Seven, as crazy as this may sound, Babe made the last out of the Series when he was caught stealing at second base. It is the only time the World Series has ended on such a play. Interestingly, even though he was pretty stocky, the Babe somehow managed to steal 123 bases during his career.

In 1927, with the help of the legendary "Murderers' Row" Yankees, one of the best teams of all time, Babe broke the single season home run record (which he had set in 1921 with 59 dingers) when he hit 60 home runs. That year, the Yankees won the World Series, and they did it again in 1928. Ruth continued to post great numbers through the years.

In 1932, at the age of 37, in the third game of the 1932 World Series against the Chicago Cubs at Wrigley Field, Ruth took two called strikes from pitcher Charlie Root, and then, with the count at two balls and two strikes, legend says he pointed to center field as if to say "I'm gonna hit the next pitch into those seats," and … he did!! The "Called Shot" is one of the most hotly debated stories in baseball history, though Ruth himself said it was true.

In the first ever All Star Game, on July 6, 1933, at Comiskey Park in Chicago, home of the White Sox, the Babe hit the first ever All Star game homer.

By the time he retired with the Boston Braves in the middle of the 1935 season, Babe Ruth had hit an amazing 714 homers, driven in 2,214 runs, scored 2,174 runs, and had a lifetime batting average of .342. He still has the all-time record for highest career slugging percentage at a whopping .690! (Slugging percentage is the single best statistic to measure a batter's power, calculated by dividing total bases by at bats. A slugging percentage of .500 for a season is very good.) The last honor he received in his unparalled career was to be one of the first five players elected into the National Baseball Hall of Fame in 1936, along with Christy Mathewson, Walter Johnson, Ty Cobb and Honus Wagner (for more on the Hall of Fame, check out "Hallowed Hall"). When he retired, he led baseball in career homers and RBIs and held countless other offensive records. Honestly, when Ruth retired, he led baseball in career popularity, kid fan support, and just overall greatness. Although he died in 1948 from cancer, his legend will never die, simply because he was the greatest baseball player who ever lived.

Cantankerous Cobb

Ty Cobb

Although this player is considered one of the meanest Hall of Famers in the history of baseball, he is still the best hitter based on batting average that the game has ever seen. In case you don't know him, his name is Ty Cobb. Shortly after the death of his dad, Ty debuted in center field for the Detroit Tigers, at the tender age of 18. On August 30, 1905, he played in his first major league game and doubled off the New York Highlanders' Jack Chesbro, winner of 41 games the season before. Cobb was the youngest player in the league, yet he was brought back to the club for 1906.

The ever-observant Ty Cobb.

In 1906, Cobb became the Tigers' full-time center fielder and he hit .316, his lowest average from that point until the end of his career.

Ty always slid to win.

Cobb was extremely competitive and would do just about anything to win, which included being especially aggressive on the base paths.

Cobb was so despised that in 1910 another team actually tried to let another opposing player beat Cobb for the batting title. Towards the end of the season, Cobb led Napoleon Lajoie for the American League batting title. However, in the last two games of the Cleveland Naps' season, a doubleheader against the St. Louis Browns (the current Baltimore Orioles), Browns third baseman, Red Corriden, played very far behind the third base bag when Lajoie was up to bat because his manager told him to do so. Lajoie went 8-9 in the double header, with six bunt singles towards third base. Even with all this going on to help Lajoie, The Sporting News declared Cobb the winner of the 1910 batting title with a .385 average for Cobb as compared to a .384 average for Lajoie. However, 70 years later it was determined that Cobb had been incorrectly credited with two extra hits in 1910, so Cobb's average was revised down to .383, but the Commissioner at the time ruled not to take away Cobb's 1910 batting title.

"Cobb regarded baseball as 'something like a war,'" fellow Tiger Hall of Famer Charlie Gehringer said. "Every time at bat for him was a crusade." Baseball historian John Thorn has said, "He is testament to how far you can get simply through will . . . Cobb was pursued by demons."

In 1911, Cobb had an amazing .420 average (his career high) with a 40-game hitting streak! He was in the middle of a run during which he won nine straight batting titles, and 12 overall in his career. That year he led the league in virtually every offensive category except for home runs. He also won his only MVP award that year. By the way, the following year Cobb slumped and only batted .409!!

All in all, the "Georgia Peach" may have been baseball's greatest average hitter and most intense competitor, but he never won a World Series. His batting accomplishments during his 24 year career are legendary, including a lifetime average of .366, 295 triples, 724 doubles, 897 stolen bases, 2,246 runs scored, 1,938 runs batted in and 4,189 hits (second all time to Pete Rose's 4,256). So even without a World Series title, Ty still had one of the greatest careers ever.

Cobb's Counterpart

While Ty Cobb was tearing up AL pitching, in the National League Honus Wagner was nearly as great a hitting machine. One of the Hall of Fame's five original inductees in 1936, along with Cobb, "The Flying Dutchman" was excellent offensively and defensively in a 21-year career. The longtime Pirates shortstop broke into baseball by hitting .335 in 1897 with Louisville, the first of 16 seasons of hitting over .300, including eight as the National League's batting champ. Wagner had a lifetime average of .328 with 3,420 career hits, and he also stole 723 bases, while leading the league in that category five times.

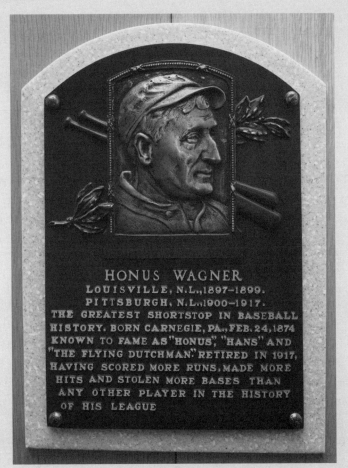

Honus Wagner, one of the legendary first five Hall of Fame inductees.

Dynamic Dodgers

The Brooklyn and Los Angeles Dodgers

There are two teams that usually come to mind when you think of the World Series: the Dodgers and the Yankees. These two teams have met eleven times in the World Series, with the Yankees winning eight. But that doesn't alter the fact that the Dodgers probably have the richest history of any NL team.

The Brooklyn Dodgers (who, before 1932, also went by names like the Atlantics, the Superbas, the Grays, the Bridegrooms and the Robins), were formed in 1884. Their first World Series appearance came in 1916, which they lost to the Boston Red Sox. In fact, their first and only World Series championship in Brooklyn, New York didn't come until 1955! Wait, let's back up a little bit.

After decades of mediocrity, in the 1940s, following the hiring of Branch Rickey as general manager, the Dodgers began to improve, getting future Hall of Famers Duke Snider, Roy Campanella, Pee Wee Reese, and of course, Jackie Robinson, the player who broke the color barrier. They also had the great first baseman Gil Hodges. Their greatest success in Brooklyn came in the 1950s when they won four pennants and, led by manager Walter Alston, their only championship in 1955, with the New York Yankees taking the title in all the other Series.

After 1957, the Dodgers crushed the hearts of their local fans when they moved to Los Angeles, becoming the first team to be on the west coast. In 1959, with some of their Hall of Famers retired, they still managed

Jackie Robinson steals home against the Yankees.

to get to the World Series to face the Chicago White Sox. They actually ended up winning that one, and the one four years later as well, in
1963, with the help of the legendary left-handed pitcher Sandy Koufax,
the Jewish New Yorker who finally reached his true potential, winning
25 games that season and the World Series MVP. Sandy, in fact, was so
good during his career, that he earned the nickname of "the Left Hand
of God." He won the World Series MVP award again in 1965, leading
the Dodgers to a seven game victory over the Minnesota Twins. Koufax
also won three Cy Young Awards during his career, back when only one
award was given out for all of MLB (for more on the Cy Young Award,
check out "Yeoman Young").

The 1970s was another strong decade for the Dodgers, led by a gaggle
of great infielders, Steve Garvey, Ron Cey, Bill Russell and Davey Lopes,

along with manager Tommy Lasorda. The four infielders played together longer than any other quartet in baseball history. The Dodgers of this

The "Left Hand of God," Sandy Koufax.

era had great pitching as well, including Don Sutton, Tommy John and Charlie Hough. They got to back-to-back World Series in 1977 and '78, but lost both to the Yankees. However, they went back to the World Series in 1981 against the Yanks (again) and beat them in six. Finally, in 1988, inspired by a walk-off Game One home run off the bat of severely injured Kirk Gibson, as well as the tremendous pitching of Orel Hershiser throughout the Series, the Dodgers bashed the Bash Brothers and the rest of the Oakland A's in five games.

In all, the Dodgers have appeared in 18 World Series, the second most of any NL team (to the Cardinals' and Giants' 19 each). However, their six championships rank only sixth all-time. They have many Hall of Famers, including Don Drysdale, Don Sutton, Sandy Koufax, Jackie Robinson and Zack Wheat. Although the Dodgers' biggest National League rival has always been the Giants, it's safe to say that the Dodgers have a "giant" legacy.

Excruciating Errors

Famous Errors in Baseball History

Errors are just a part of baseball, but sometimes they can come back to haunt you. Most errors involve a defensive player making a fielding mistake, allowing a runner to reach base when he should have been out. All players make errors, even the greatest defensive stars of all time, like Ozzie Smith and Brooks Robinson. Yes, errors are part of the game, but an error at the wrong time can mean the difference between winning and losing.

The Mets celebrate their improbable 1986 Series win.

In the 1984 National League Championship Series, Cubs first baseman Leon Durham made an error that allowed two unearned runs to score in the bottom of the seventh inning of the fifth and deciding game, which the San Diego Padres won 6-3. The

Padres went on to the World Series, which eventually they lost to the Detroit Tigers in five games.

Another huge error occurred in the 2009 National League Divisional Series, when Cardinals left fielder Matt Holliday dropped a fly ball hit by James Loney with two outs in the ninth and his team leading 2-1. If Holliday had caught the ball, the series would have been tied 1-1. But instead, Loney reached base and the momentum propelled the Dodgers to a dramatic 3-2 comeback victory! That was the turning point in the series, as the Los Angeles Dodgers went on to win the series and go on to the NLCS.

In Game Four of the 1941 World Series, the Brooklyn Dodgers were up by one run with two strikes on Tommy Henrich of the Yankees in the ninth. If catcher Mickey Owen had caught the third strike, the World Series would have been tied at two games apiece, but he dropped the ball and Henrich reached first! The Yankees went on to score four runs in the inning and eventually won the Series a couple of days later.

In the bottom of the tenth at Shea Stadium with the Red Sox up against the Mets 5-3 in Game Six of the 1986 World Series, the Mets were down to their final strike of the Series, but they came back. After three singles, the score was 5-4 Red Sox with runners on first and third with Mookie Wilson at the plate. On a 2-2 count, Red Sox pitcher Bob Stanley threw a wild pitch to bring the tying run in and move the winning run on first, Ray Knight, to second. A few pitches later, Wilson hit a ground ball towards first baseman Bill Buckner...and it went right through his legs!!!! The Mets won the game and went on to win the Series, as the Curse of the Bambino was kept alive.

Another very famous error occurred during the final game of the 1912 World Series between the Boston Red Sox and the New York Giants. It was the bottom of the tenth inning with the Giants up 2-1 and the Red Sox at the plate. Clyde Engle of the Sox was hitting and he lifted a routine fly ball to center field. Giants center fielder Fred Snodgrass was there to make what should have been an easy catch, but he just dropped it! This "muff," as it later was called, allowed Engle to reach second base and eventually score on a Tris Speaker single. A few batters later, the Red Sox won the World Series on a sacrifice fly. Had Snodgrass made the catch in center, the Giants would've won the Series, but unfortunately for Giants fans, that did not happen.

Sometimes, though, even making a lot of errors is not held against a player. "Rabbit" Maranville had 65 errors in 1914 and yet was second in the MVP vote and, more importantly, even though he holds the 20th century record for career errors with 711, he was nonetheless elected to the Hall of Fame in 1954 for the positive things he did during his 23 year career, from 1912-1935.

Errors can happen to anyone at any time, and make up a big part of baseball lore. You never know when a routine play can go topsy turvy, and change history forever.

Fabulous Fields

Fenway Park and Wrigley Field

There have been many "cathedrals" in baseball. Today some have a modern, family-friendly look, and some are as legendary as Yankee Stadium. However, two of today's ballparks stand out from all the rest. These ballparks are historic in many ways, but are probably most famous for

Fenway Park in all its glory.

housing their famous teams, the Boston Red Sox and Chicago Cubs, who make their homes in, respectively, Fenway Park and Wrigley Field.

Fenway Park, named because it was built on marshy grounds (a fen is an old English word for marsh), has been the home of the Boston Red Sox since 1912. It is the oldest standing ballpark in Major League Baseball and features some of the most interesting and quirky features in all of ballpark history, including The Triangle, Pesky's Pole and, most notably, the Green Monster, the 37-foot high left field wall, the tallest in ballpark history. The park itself has hosted 11 World Series, from 1912, which the Red Sox won over the Giants, to Boston's most recent, a win over the St. Louis Cardinals in 2013.

In 2008, the park sold out its 456th consecutive Red Sox game, breaking the Major League Baseball record that had been set by the Cleveland Indians. Fenway has also been the setting for numerous great moments in baseball history, including:

- The deciding game of the 1912 World Series, when Fred Snodgrass's muffed fly ball gives the Red Sox new life in the bottom of the tenth against the Giants, a game the Red Sox went on to win on a walk-off sacrifice fly.

- September 28, 1960, in a game against the Baltimore Orioles, the legendary Ted Williams launches a home run in the last at bat of his career.

- Game Six of the 1975 World Series ends with a bang, as Hall of Fame catcher Carlton Fisk hits a walk-off homer off the left field foul pole, ending perhaps the greatest game in World Series history, and setting up a dramatic Game Seven that would be, sadly for Red Sox fans, won by the visiting Cincinnati Reds. The image of Fisk waving his ball fair is one of the most famous in baseball history.

- The 1978 one-game playoff to decide the winner of the AL East is won by the Yankees, thanks to timely homers by Reggie Jackson and, especially, Bucky Dent.

Fans always flock to Wrigley Field.

- At the 1999 All Star Game, with the all-century team in attendance, Ted Williams does something he had rarely done as a player: He tipped his cap to the fans.

Although Fenway Park is arguably the most legendary ballpark ever, there is one that comes in a close second. This park is one of the most recognizable baseball fields, because of its interesting outfield wall. The ballpark is none other than Wrigley Field.

The stadium was built in 1914 for the Chicago Whales for the Federal League baseball team (a league that wasn't part of the majors), and called Weeghman Park. It was then called Cubs Park before being renamed for the team's owner at the time, William Wrigley Jr. (the chewing gum man). Wrigley Field has been home to the Cubs since 1916, and is also home to the fans called "Bleacher Bums" who sit beyond left field and are famous for their constant heckling.

Wrigley Field sits on one of the biggest intersections on the north side of the Windy City. The area surrounding the ballpark contains houses and restaurants, a neighborhood people call "Wrigleyville." You can even watch games from the rooftops of buildings across the street from Wrigley Field!! How cool is that?

"Mr. Cub," Hall of Famer Ernie Banks, frequently referred to Wrigley Field as the "The Friendly Confines," a name that stuck. It is the oldest National League ballpark and the second oldest overall, after Fenway. In fact, lighting wasn't installed at the park until 1988!! Wrigley is best known for its very cool ivy-covered brick outfield wall (which has led to many fielding adventures over the years) and its hand-turned scoreboard.

Although Wrigley Field has been the home of the Cubs since 1916, it has yet to see the Cubs win a World Series, even though it has hosted a whole bunch of them (1929, 1932, 1935, 1938 and 1945, the last time, amazingly, the Cubs appeared in the World Series). The Cubs last won a World Series way back in 1908, before Wrigley Field even existed. However, even though it lacks championships, Wrigley Field is still a ballpark for the ages.

Baseball is a game of traditions, and nowhere are those traditions felt more strongly than at Fenway Park and Wrigley Field, two ball fields that will always have a place in baseball history.

Golden Gloves

The Greatest Defensive Players Ever

The Rawlings Gold Glove Award is awarded each year to the player in each league who is the best at fielding his specific position. Many Hall of Famers are Hall of Famers mainly because of their sparkling defensive play. That's right, not all Hall of Famers were great hitters. Some are famous for their glove.

Brooks Robinson, the "Human Vacuum Cleaner," sucks in another ball.

The Gold Glove Award was given out for the first time in 1957, although separate awards were not awarded to the American and National Leagues until the next season. In 1957, Willie Mays finally received official recognition for his amazing defense when he was named the Gold Glove winner for center field. The "Say Hey Kid" continued to win Gold Gloves, winning the next eleven years in a row!! In that time period equally awesome defensive excellence was shown by Roberto Clemente who, with a cannon-like throwing arm, won 12 straight Gold Gloves from 1961 to 1972.

Willie Mays unleashes a bullet.

In the AL, third baseman Brooks Robinson (aka "The Human Vacuum Cleaner") of the Orioles was the most prominent superstar fielder, collecting 16 straight Gold Gloves from 1960-1975. A pair of pitchers stole the show for fielding in the AL, Jim Kaat of the Twins (who won the first 14) and Jim Palmer of the Orioles (who won the next four). From 1962-1979, no other pitchers won American League Gold Gloves except for those two.

The '80s were dominated by Keith Hernandez and Ozzie ("The Wizard") Smith. Hernandez helped the Mets win their second title in '86 with his great fielding at first base, and collected 11 Gold Gloves in his career, while the shortstop Smith used his wizardry in the field, winning 13 consecutive Gold Gloves, from 1980-1992, and making plays never seen before at the position (not to mention his somersaults between innings).

Many other great fielders took home multiple awards, like Garry Maddox (the "Secretary of Defense"), who won eight Gold Gloves as an outfielder for the Phillies. Hall of Fame pitcher Greg Maddux did even better, winning 18 career Gold Gloves, an MLB record for any position. Catcher Johnny Bench's powerful arm helped him win ten consecutive Gold Gloves with the Reds, while Ken Griffey Jr. amazed Seattle Mariners fans with ten Gold Gloves of his own in the outfield. Ivan Rodriguez is also very famous for winning Gold Gloves, having collected a record 13 as a catcher for an assortment of teams.

Although some of these players are not in the Hall of Fame, baseball fans remember them for their excellence in the field. Some were not even the best of hitters, like Ozzie Smith, who batted .262 in his career. However, they are all still great, and were very valuable to their teams because they fielded with "golden gloves."

Hallowed Hall

The Baseball Hall of Fame

Ten baseball Hall of Famers pose outside the museum in Cooperstown, June 12, 1939. Front row: Eddie Collins, Babe Ruth, Connie Mack, Cy Young. Back row: Honus Wagner, Grover Cleveland Alexander, Tris Speaker, Napoleon Lajoie, George Sisler and Walter Johnson.

The National Baseball Hall of Fame and Museum is a place where fans can experience the excitement of all the greatest people (the Hall of Famers) who played or were involved with the game of baseball. Only the greatest players, managers, umpires, executives and pioneers get elected to be members of the Hall of Fame. The museum is located in a small town in upstate New York called Cooperstown. The reason that the Hall is located in this small town of just about 2,000 is because when the museum opened, many believed that baseball was invented there. The Hall of Fame is a symbol of excellence for all baseball players from the major leagues down to Little League. It is a source of hope and inspiration, as kids who walk down the Hall's halls admire the greats and think to themselves that one day they might be the next Willie Stargell or Nolan Ryan. The Hall is also a great place for fans of all ages and interests to come and admire the stars of the game's past and learn about its rich history.

The Hall's fabled plaque room.

The National Baseball Hall of Fame and Museum opened its doors in 1939, although the first ever class was elected in 1936 (which included Babe Ruth, Ty Cobb, Christy Mathewson, Walter Johnson and Honus Wagner). Out of those five, Cobb got the most votes, due in part to his having the highest batting average of all time at .366, a record that still stands. An important thing to note is that Ruth was inducted into the Hall a year after his retirement, but today a ballplayer generally must be retired for five years before becoming eligible to appear on the voting ballot. Once on the ballot, the player has 10 years to get elected into Cooperstown by being named on at least 75% of sportswriters' ballots (the Baseball Writers Association of America). If he doesn't get elected in those 10 years, then the Veterans Committee may still induct him.

In 1937, the winningest pitcher in baseball history (511 wins!!) Denton True "Cy" Young, was inducted into the heralded Hall. Also elected that year were baseball's two greatest managers of the time, Connie Mack of the Athletics, who was actually still managing, and John McGraw of the Giants. In 1939, Lou Gehrig became a member of the Hall of Fame, even though he had only retired earlier that year, because sometimes exceptions to the five year retirement rule are made for special cases like Gehrig and Roberto Clemente, who both tragically passed away in their 30's.

Other all-time greats gaining admission include Jimmie Foxx, in 1951, having retired with the second-most homers in baseball history at the time with 534. Four years later, "Joltin" Joe DiMaggio (owner of the longest consecutive game hitting streak ever at 56 games) had his name etched in baseball history. In 1966, Ted Williams and Casey Stengel got into the Hall, two legends from rival teams. In 1971, Satchel Paige became the first former Negro Leaguer to get into the Hall of Fame. Since then, 25 more Negro Leaguers have been inducted into Cooperstown. As a matter of fact, Ted Williams' induction speech made a case for Paige and other great Negro Leagues players, and started the momentum to getting him and others elected.

As the years went by, all of baseball's greatest stars got into the Hall including Hank Aaron, Willie Mays, Mickey Mantle, Duke Snider, Warren Spahn, Reggie Jackson, George Brett, Mike Schmidt, Carl Yastrzemski, Carlton Fisk, Willie McCovey, Eddie Mathews and so many more.

A major event happened at the Hall of Fame in 2006 when Effa Manley became the first ever woman inducted into the Hall of Fame. She was a very influential executive in the Negro Leagues with the Newark Eagles and was also a great civil rights crusader. Manley was elected as part of the Special Committee on the Negro Leagues, a special group formed by the Veterans Committee focusing on the Negro Leagues. Along with Manley, 16 other Negro Leaguers were inducted via the SCNL.

Effa Manley, the first female elected to the Hall of Fame.

The Hall currently has over 300 members, which is a pretty small number considering that over 20,000 people have played or otherwise been involved with Major League Baseball. Clearly, it is a very exclusive club. The bottom line is that Hall of Fame members are the best of the best in baseball history. Period. End of story.

Hall Hopefuls

One of the most enjoyable discussions baseball fans have is which current players will get into the Hall of Fame. Among active players, several are sure things, while with others, we will just have to wait and see.

Albert Pujols has over 500 home runs and he hasn't even played 15 years in the big leagues yet. Derek Jeter is the all-time Yankees hits leader with 3,465, he captained the Yankees and has five World Series rings. Ichiro Suzuki won Rookie of the Year and MVP in 2001, has over 4,000 hits combined between his American and Japanese League baseball careers, and has a career MLB batting average near .320. Miguel Cabrera is only 31, but he has already won two MVP awards, a Triple Crown, and is approaching 400 home runs.

There are also several young players in the big leagues who, if they keep doing what they've done so far, will also likely get into the Hall of Fame. Clayton Kershaw has a career ERA under 3.00, along with three Cy Young Awards and an MVP award in his first seven seasons. Mike Trout (leaping on this book's cover), still in his early 20's, has won one MVP award and come in second twice in his first three years in the majors. Craig Kimbrel won the Rookie of the Year Award in his first season and has led the National League in saves for the past four seasons.

Incredible Iron Horse

Lou Gehrig

Lou Gehrig belts one.

Of all the players in baseball history, none has possessed such a magnificent combination of talent and humility as Lou Gehrig. The strong and humble star is one of the best baseball has ever seen, and his story is one of the most dramatic of all time. Gehrig was born on June 19, 1903 in New York City, the son of German immigrants. His mother, Christina, worked tirelessly, cooking, cleaning houses and taking in laundry to make ends meet. His father, Heinrich, often had trouble finding work and was in poor health. Christina wanted young Lou to get a good education, so in 1921 Lou's parents sent him to Columbia University for college. Gehrig was a fullback at Columbia during the 1922 football season, and the next year pitched and played first base for the baseball team. When baseball scout Paul Krichell saw the Columbia baseball team play, Gehrig's hitting skills impressed him so much that he signed Gehrig to play for the Yankees. After a full season with one of the Yankee minor league teams, in Hartford, Connecticut, where Gehrig hit .369, he became a Yankee for good in 1925. Once he replaced Wally Pipp at first base because of a ball that hit Pipp's head, Gehrig amazingly did not miss a game for the next 13 years.

Gehrig's consecutive game streak of 2,130 games (a record that stood until Baltimore Orioles legendary shortstop Cal Ripken, Jr. broke it in 1995) did not come easily. He played well every day, even though he had many bad injuries during his career. For example, one day, despite having a serious lower back injury, Gehrig was listed as the shortstop and leadoff hitter. He singled and was promptly replaced, but the streak was kept alive. His endurance and strength earned him the nickname the "Iron Horse."

After batting .295 in 1925, the next year Gehrig hit .313 and led the league with 20 triples. This was the first of 12 consecutive seasons he would top .300. The Yankees won the pennant and Gehrig hit a solid .348 in the World Series, but the Yankees lost to the Cardinals in seven games. The next year, 1927, would be a magical year for Gehrig.

Babe Ruth and Gehrig began to dominate the baseball headlines in 1927 in a way two players had never done before. That year Ruth hit 60 homers, breaking his own record of 59, and Gehrig hit 47 home runs, a career high (and second in history at the time to only Ruth), with a whopping 173 runs batted in. Together they out-homered every team in baseball except one. The Yanks went on to win the World Series that year and Gehrig won the MVP (his first of two).

Ruth often overshadowed Gehrig during his career, but Lou was fine with that. He was a private person who enjoyed his success quietly. Even after Ruth left the Yanks, Joe DiMaggio quickly filled the paparazzi void.

In his excellent career, Lou's lifetime batting average was .340, 15th on the all-time list. Also, Gehrig averaged a mammoth 142 RBIs per 154 game season.

A pensive "Iron Horse."

Gehrig won the Triple Crown in 1934, with a .363 average, 49 homers and 166 RBI. Believe it or not, he came in only fifth in the MVP voting that year, which was won by Mickey Cochrane of the Tigers, but he was chosen Most Valuable Player again in 1936. That year, and the next three, the Yankees won four straight World Series, though Gehrig was not part of the one in '39.

At the beginning of the 1939 season, Gehrig fell into a major slump. His skills had suddenly eroded. On May 2, 1939, he took himself out of the lineup, ending his streak of 2,130 consecutive games played. Soon, he was diagnosed with Amyotrophic Lateral Sclerosis, or ALS, a disease with no cure. Gehrig retired during the season, and that year was inducted into the Hall of Fame. Sadly, in June of 1941, Lou passed away at age 37. His loss was deeply mourned. Lou had an incredible career, and now even non-sports fans know his name, as the deadly disease that took his life is commonly referred to as "Lou Gehrig's Disease." Although he was very sick at the end of his career, he considered himself "the luckiest man on the face of the earth."

Juggernaut Johnson

Walter Johnson

Some say Cy Young was the greatest pitcher of all time. While Cy Young has the most career wins with 511, a certain Washington Senator who has the career record for shutouts is generally considered to be the best pitcher ever. This person had over 400 wins, 417 to be precise, despite pitching for some pretty bad teams. This pitcher is named Walter Johnson, and you will see soon enough why he is viewed as the greatest pitcher ever.

Walter "Big Train" Johnson established several amazing pitching records during his storied career. In addition to being the all-time leader in shutouts with 110, and ranking second in wins, he was the all-time strikeout leader (at 3,509) for over 50 years, and he led the league

The greatest pitcher of all time, Walter Johnson.

in strikeouts an astounding 12 times!! (For more about strikeouts, check out the next chapter.)

During his career, Johnson had twelve 20 win seasons, including two of more than 30! Another amazing accomplishment is that on September 4, 5 and 7, 1908, he shut out the New York Highlanders in three consecutive games.

Johnson won the Triple Crown for pitchers three times, meaning he led the league in wins, ERA, and strikeouts (for more about pitching Triple Crowns, check out "Triumphant Trifectas"). And his career ERA was a miniscule 2.17, the 12th best of all-time! By the way, ERA stands for earned run average, that is, how many earned runs a pitcher allows on average over nine innings. Nowadays, if a pitcher has an ERA of 3.00, he's considered pretty great.

One of Johnson's greatest feats was when, in 1913, he pitched 55 2/3 consecutive scoreless innings, which is still the American League record.

Towards the end of his career, in 1924, Johnson finally led the Senators to the Fall Classic against the Giants. While he lost his first two games despite pitching well, he became the Series hero by pitching four score-less relief innings in the deciding seventh game, which the Senators won in 12 innings. His team returned to the World Series the next year, but this time Johnson lost game seven to give the championship to the Pi-rates, after having won games one and four.

Johnson was considered a very nice person and everyone liked him. This made his fan support huge. Given all that he did and how he acted, both on and off the field, it was no surprise that he was part of the first class to get elected into the Hall of Fame in 1936. See, that's how real baseball is played: no fights, just great plays.

Junior Juggernaut

Walter Johnson is the only person with the last name "Johnson" currently in the Hall of Fame, but another Johnson, namely Randy, will be appearing on the ballot in 2015, and is expected to join Walter in the Hall soon. While Walter and Randy are not known to be related, they share the traits of being dominant pitchers and strikeout kings. Randy "The Big Unit" Johnson played from 1988-2009 with the Expos, Mariners, Diamondbacks, Yankees, Astros and Giants. He won an astounding five Cy Young Awards (and came in second three times), the last four awards coming consecutively from 1999-2002, with the Arizona Diamondbacks. The ten-time All Star won 303 career games and only lost 166. He led the league in ERA four times and in strikeouts nine times. In fact, Randy is second on the all-time list of career strikeouts with 4,875, and is first on the list among lefthanders.

Randy Johnson about to fire a pitch home.

Kings of K

The Greatest Strikeout Pitchers Ever

One of the most important statistics for pitchers is the strikeout. Simply put, a strikeout occurs when a batter collects three strikes during an at bat, after which the batter is declared out. A strike is either a ball that is pitched into the strike zone or a pitch that a batter swings at but misses. Now, it's time to pay homage to some of the best strikeout pitchers in baseball history.

Nolan Ryan

The intense Nolan Ryan.

Ryan is the all-time leader in strikeouts with 5,714, almost 1,000 more than the man with the second most, Randy Johnson. Lynn Nolan Ryan was able to overpower hitters throughout his 27-year career (until he retired at age 46) with his amazing fastball, reaching speeds over 100 miles per hour. In addition, he had an overpowering curveball to go along with it. Because of his pitching speed, Nolan was dubbed the "Ryan Express." His amazing ability to strike out batters allowed him to pitch a record seven no-hitters during his career, spent with the Mets, Angels, Astros and Rangers. He also holds records with 363 games with at least 10 strikeouts and 383 strikeouts in a season. The eight-time All Star won 324 games during his career and was inducted into the Hall of Fame in his first year of eligibility in 1999 with 98.8% of the vote.

Steve Carlton

Another legend on the all-time strikeouts list is Steve "Lefty" Carlton. Lefty collected 4,136 career punchouts in 24 years, mainly with the Cardinals and Phillies. Unlike Ryan, whose fastball was his best pitch, Carlton would regularly confuse hitters with his vir-

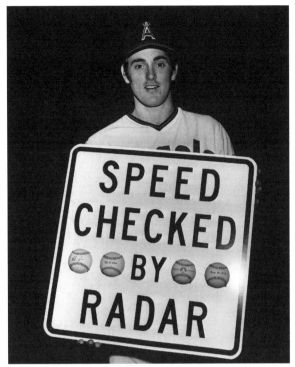

Boy, could the "Ryan Express" throw fast!

tually unhittable slider. That slider helped him win 329 games during his Hall of Fame career. That win total is second to only Warren Spahn when it comes to lefties. The first ever four-time Cy Young Award winner struck out 19 batters in a 1969 game with the Cardinals against the Mets, but he still lost the game 4-3. He led the league in strikeouts five times and was part of the Phillies' two NL pennant-winning teams in 1980 and 1983.

Bob Gibson

Bob "Hoot" Gibson was the second pitcher in baseball history to record more than 3,000 strikeouts in his career (the first was Walter Johnson). To be specific, in 17 years with the Cardinals, Gibby struck out 3,117 batters. The always intimidating two-time Cy Young Award winner had a 2.91 career ERA, including a microscopic 1.12 ERA in 1968 (the lowest in MLB since the early 1900's), the year in which he won both the

The intimidating Bob Gibson.

Cy Young Award and NL MVP. His 17 strikeouts in Game One of the 1968 World Series is still a record today, and he also set a World Series record by winning seven consecutive complete game decisions.

Tom Seaver

The player with the highest vote percentage in Hall of Fame history (at 98.84%) is this great pitcher, George Thomas Seaver, better known as Tom or "Tom Terrific." During Seaver's stellar career, he helped lead the Miracle Mets to the 1969 World Series championship by posting a 25-7 record and collecting the first of his three Cy Young awards. Tom also pitched for the Reds, White Sox and Red Sox and struck out 3,640 batters during his career, leading his league for five seasons in that category. Tom finished his 20-year career with a lifetime record of 311-205, an amazing 106 games over .500, despite having pitched on mediocre teams for a large part of his career. He certainly was terrific!

Legendary Legs

The Greatest Base Stealers Ever

In baseball, singles, doubles, triples, homers, errors, and great fielding plays aren't the only ways to make something exciting happen in a game. Sometimes, you just have to use your legs and "steal a base." A stolen base is when a runner is able to advance safely to the next base without the ball being put in play, usually while the pitcher is throwing the ball to home plate. Some baseball players are great because they have power or hit for a high average, but there are a number of Hall of Famers who made it mainly on the strength of their stolen base skills.

Rickey Henderson racking up the stolen bases.

One of the greatest base stealers in baseball history, "Larcenous" Lou Brock, helped to completely change the approach to stealing by focusing on the science of it and studying pitchers' weaknesses. He totaled 938 stolen bases in his 19-year career with the Cubs and Cardinals, from 1961-1979. The six-time All Star stole an average of 58 bags per year, including 118 bases in 1974, then the all-time re-cord. He is tied for the most stolen bases in World Series play at 14 with Eddie Collins, and every year the National League honors its stolen base leader with the Lou Brock Award.

Hall of Famer Frankie "The Fordham Flash" Frisch was not as active of a base stealer as Brock, but he still managed to steal 419 in his 19-year career with the Giants and Cardinals, from 1919-1937. His single season high in the category was 49 stolen bases in 1921, which led the league. He led the league in stolen bases three times and won the NL MVP in 1931, the last year he led the league in SB's, with 28.

"The Man of Steal." That's all one needs to say when describing Rickey Henderson. He is the most prolific base stealer the game has ever seen. His 1,406 career SB's from 1979-2003, with an abundance of teams, is a record that will likely never be broken, and his 130 stolen bases in 1982 is also a modern day record for one season (Hugh Nicol actually stole 138 bases back in 1887). Henderson led the American League in steals 12 times. He also holds the record for times caught stealing with 335.

How do you suppose Henderson got all those stolen bases? With his more than 3,000 hits and the all-time record for unintentional walks with 2,129, Henderson is also considered the greatest leadoff batter of all time. In addition, because he was the master of stealing third base (324 times), it helped him set the all-time career record of 2,295 runs scored!! Lastly, he hit a ton of homers for a leadoff hitter (297), including a record 81 to lead off games, and won the 1990 AL MVP award.

Other stolen base legends include: Tim Raines, who over a 23-year career stole 808 bases, at a very high 84.7% success rate; Max Carey, who led his league in steals ten times and stole 738 bases in total from 1910-1929; Billy Hamilton, who batted .344 lifetime and swiped 914 bases from 1888-1901, including four seasons with 100 or more steals; Luis Aparicio, who totaled 506 career steals and led the AL during the first nine years of his career; and two-time MVP Joe Morgan, who stole 689 bases from 1963-1984.

Magnificent Mays

Willie Mays

Willie Mays playing stickball, and working on his game.

A five-tool player in baseball is someone who can hit, hit for power, run, field and throw. No one displayed those skills better than the "Say Hey Kid," Willie Mays. A 24-time All Star and two-time MVP, who totaled 660 career home runs, a .302 lifetime batting average, 1,903 RBI, 2,062 runs, 338 stolen bases, 3,283 hits and 12 Gold Gloves, nobody did it better overall than Willie Mays. Interestingly, Mays has attributed his hitting success to his ability to hit the breaking ball, which he honed through many hours spent playing stickball on the streets of Harlem, New York during the early part of his MLB career.

Willie started playing professional baseball in the Negro Leagues just after Jackie Robinson broke the color barrier, but soon got to the majors

Another homer for the "Say Hey Kid."

with the New York Giants in 1951. After going hitless in his first 12 at bats, he homered on his "lucky" 13th at bat off future Hall of Famer Warren Spahn. Mays won the 1951 Rookie of the Year Award belting 20 homers and driving in 68 runs. The Giants reached the World Series that year, but lost to the Yankees.

Mays went to the Army for 1952 and 1953, but he came back swinging in 1954 with a .345 average and 41 home runs. He won the NL MVP award and then, in the World Series, Mays made what is known simply as "The Catch," leading the Giants to a memorable sweep against the heavily favored Cleveland Indians, in one of the biggest upsets ever (for more on Mays' catch, check out "Unbelievable Underdogs").

Mays continued to excel in 1955 and 1956, hitting 51 home runs one year, and becoming the first NL player to have over 30 homers and 30 steals in a season the next. Then, as mentioned earlier in this book, in 1957, the first season the Gold Glove was presented, Mays won the first of his 12 consecutive awards.

After the 1957 season, the Giants moved to San Francisco, California, where Mays continued to be one of baseball's very best. The Giants won the National League pennant in 1962, with Mays leading the team in eight offensive categories (including 49 home runs, 141 runs batted in and 130 runs), but the Giants lost to the Yankees in the Series, Mays' last World Series appearance as a member of the Giants.

Mays continued to post great numbers throughout his career and eventually got to a final World Series in 1973 with the New York Mets, but they lost to the Athletics in seven games. However, it really didn't matter what happened in that Series or in any other, because no matter what, Willie Mays is the greatest all-around baseball player of all time.

No Comparison
New York Yankees

The Yankee Dynasty

The Yankees have the winningest and most amazing history of any team in Major League Baseball (or any American sport for that matter). So let's start from the beginning.

The Bambino could have a whole museum wing, not just a plaque.

In 1901, the American League was created. In that league was the newly-formed Baltimore Orioles, who moved to New York in 1903 and became known as the New York Highlanders. They played at Hilltop Park, but they weren't very good, managing just five seasons above .500 from 1901-1918. Then on December 26, 1919, the Red Sox sold Babe Ruth to the newly-renamed Yankees, and everything changed. The Yankees became a powerhouse and never looked back. They won three straight pennants from 1921-1923. In 1923, because of the popularity of Babe Ruth, the Yankees were able to move into Yankee Stadium, a

Joltin' Joe en route to 56 straight.

cathedral of a ballpark. Thus, the moniker "the house that Ruth built."

In the first year in the new stadium, the Yanks won their first World Series, against the Giants in six games. After a loss in the Series in 1926, the "Murderers Row" 1927 Yankees exploded out of the gate for one of the best seasons ever. They won 111 games, with Babe Ruth hitting 60 homers, a record at the time, while Lou Gehrig hit 47. The Yanks batted just under .300 as a team and swept the Pirates in the World Series.

Not long after championships in 1928 and 1932, The Babe retired and was replaced by future Hall of Famer, Joe DiMaggio. Together Joe and Lou Gehrig continued to slaughter AL pitching, leading the Yankees to four straight World Series titles, from 1936-1939.

After Gehrig retired, the Yanks had a hard time recovering, but thanks to a record 56-game hitting streak by DiMaggio in the midst of the summer of 1941, the Yanks won the pennant and the World Series that year, too. Joe left for World War II, but the Yanks again won the World Series in 1943 and, when he came back, they won again in 1947. In 1949, Casey Stengel was hired as the Yankees manager and they continued their success. They won an unprecedented five consecutive World Series from 1949-1953 with the help of Hall of Famers Phil Rizzuto, Yogi Berra, Joe DiMaggio (through 1951) and Mickey Mantle (from 1951 on). After losing to the Dodgers in 1955, in 1956 the Mick had his best season ever (for more on this, check out "Triumphant Trifectas"). He also led the Yanks

The one and only Mickey Mantle.

to a World Series victory over the Dodgers. In 1961, Mickey and Roger Maris challenged Babe Ruth's single-season home run record of 60. Maris beat it with 61, while injuries slowed down the Mick, who ended the season with "only" 54. Between 1947 and 1964, the Yankees played in 15 out of 18 World Series, winning ten of them.

Let's jump to the 1970s, where in the 1977 World Series, future Hall of Famer Reggie Jackson cracked home runs on three straight pitches in Game Six, propelling the Yanks past the LA Dodgers for the title. They won the World Series again the next year too, after the incredible one-game playoff to defeat archrival Boston Red Sox, thanks to Bucky Dent's unlikely 3-run home run.

In 1996, Derek Jeter, Bernie Williams, Paul O'Neill, Andy Pettitte, Mariano Rivera, and others helped get the Yanks out of their 15-year World Series drought, defeating the Braves in six, after losing the first two. 1998 was a great year for the Yankees, as they won 114 games, at the time the most in American League history. They led the league that year in runs scored, on base percentage, ERA and just about every other category, and went on to sweep the San Diego Padres in the World Series. They continued their dominance at the end of the 1990s into the 2000s, winning the 1999 and 2000 Fall Classics against the Braves and the Mets, respectively.

After surprising losses to the Arizona Diamondbacks and Florida Marlins in the 2001 and 2003 Fall Classics, the Yanks didn't win another title until they got CC Sabathia and Mark Teixeira in 2009 (as well as a brand new Yankee Stadium) and took the 2009 World Series over the Phillies in six.

Although it's the players who did the work, the Yanks have had a very good history of managers too, including Miller Huggins, Joe McCarthy, Casey Stengel, Billy Martin, Joe Torre and Joe Girardi. Well, great teams usually do have great managers, right? So the tally so far is 27 championships and counting in 40 tries. Not too shabby.

The "Captain," Derek Jeter.

Neverending Nicknames

While no "N's" in a baseball history book should replace the New York Yankees, at the same time, a book about baseball history would not be complete if it didn't have a mention of the game's great nicknames. Baseball has been full of colorful nicknames from its very earliest days, like the Say Hey Kid, the Heater from Van Meter, the Babe, Big Train and the Iron Horse. Here's a list of some other unique baseball nicknames you may want to check out some time: Cakes, Three Finger, the Big Hurt, Sir Hugh, the Scooter, the Hoosier Thunderbolt, the Human Hairpin, Old Hoss, Gerbil, Catfish, Big Unit, Big Poison, Little Poison, Goose, Ryan Express, Mr. Steady, Le Grand Orange, the Mad Hungarian, Penguin, Captain Video, Quiz, Bones, Pencils, Double XX, Beast and Crime Dog. And that's just the tip of the iceberg, so have fun!

Outstanding Outsiders

The Negro Leagues, Nippon Professional Baseball, and the All-American Girls Professional Baseball League

Josh Gibson, the "Black Babe Ruth."

Pitching legend Satchel Paige.

Major League Baseball is the most famous baseball league in the United States. However, there have been other very famous baseball leagues in the USA and around the world that have played a major role in the game. Three of those are the Negro Leagues, Nippon Professional Baseball, and the All-American Girls Professional Baseball League.

In 1920, Rube Foster, one of the great African American pitchers of his time, organized a meeting in Kansas City, Missouri with owners of professional African American barnstorming teams, to discuss organizing into a professional league. A barnstorming team was a team that did not play in a league, but instead went all over the world to play against minor league teams and other local teams not at the major league level. In the meeting, Foster and the other owners decided to form the Negro National League, with teams in the midwestern and eastern part of the country. Soon, other African-American leagues formed in other regions, of the United States, and even in Canada and Latin America.

The Negro Leagues, like Major League Baseball, during many seasons held their own World Series. From 1924 to 1927, it featured the champion of the first Negro National League against the champion of the Eastern Colored League. The winners were the Kansas City Monarchs, the Hilldale Club, and then the Chicago American Giants in back-to-back years. After a 15-year period of no championship series of any sort, a new World Series was held from 1942 to 1948 between the champions of the second Negro National League and the Negro American League. The NNL's Homestead Grays, led by future Hall of Famers Josh Gibson and Cool Papa Bell, went to the first four of these World Series, winning two of them, in 1943 and 1944. They also defeated the Birmingham Black Barons in 1948. Other winners included the Kansas City Monarchs (1942), the Cleveland Buckeyes (1945), Effa Manley's Newark Eagles (1946), and future MLB All Star Minnie Minoso's New York Cubans (1947).

Although the Negro Leagues died out a few years after MLB finally began to admit blacks in 1947, the Negro Leagues' legacy continues. In fact, there are over 25 members of the Base-

Check out the flamingo stance!

ball Hall of Fame in Cooperstown who played at least a part of their careers in the Negro Leagues. The first inductee was Satchel Paige, who pitched professionally for nearly 40 years, including several in the major leagues, which he joined in 1948 at the age of 42. Cool Papa Bell played professionally for almost 30 years and was one of the fastest men in baseball history. And then there was the legendary catcher, Josh Gibson, who was said to have hit more home runs than Babe Ruth, which is why he is called by some the "Black Babe Ruth." Also, players like Willie Mays, Henry Aaron, Jackie Robinson, Roy Campanella and the underappreciated Larry Doby (the first African American to play in the American

Ladies played pro baseball, too.

League) started out in the Negro Leagues. So, the Negro Leagues may be long gone in the real world, but not in fans' hearts.

Similar to the Negro Leagues, Nippon Professional Baseball in Japan developed out of barnstorming. In 1934, the first professional Japanese baseball team was founded, the "Dai Nippon Tokyo Yakyu Kurabu." This actually translates to "the great Tokyo baseball club." They barnstormed the USA and were very successful, and became the inspiration for the Japanese Baseball League, which became known as Nippon Professional Baseball in 1950. Since then, baseball has become as popular in Japan, if not moreso, than it is in the United States. Just like the Negro Leagues, some Nippon Professional Baseball players have made their way to MLB. For example, Ichiro Suzuki, Hideki Matsui and Daisuke Matsuzaka all played in Japan before coming to the United States. However, perhaps the best Japanese ballplayer of all time never played in the States: Sadaharu Oh. Sadaharu played for the Yomiuri Giants for his entire 22-year NPB career, from 1959-1980. He batted a lifetime .301 with a record 868 career home runs! Some say that Josh Gibson had more than that, but official stats were not kept for many of Gibson's games, so Oh is the world career home run champion! Oh won a mind-boggling nine MVP awards and 15 home run titles while utilizing his unique "flamingo" leg kick. Also, his Giants won the Japan Series (the Japanese equivalent of the World Series) 11 times during his career. Oh is truly a champion.

Another alternate baseball league was the All-American Girls Professional Baseball League, which, despite its name, actually started as a softball league in the '40s, gradually evolving into full-fledged baseball as the skills of the women improved. The league ran through 1954. The AAGPBL was formed in 1943 to help sustain the game's popularity during World War II when so many major leaguers were not playing. League executives included Branch Rickey of the Dodgers and Philip Wrigley of the Cubs. During its history, over 600 women participated in the league and teams competed for the league's championship over 12 years. The biggest winner was the Rockford Peaches, one of the first two teams in the league. The league brought great joy to many fans, especially during wartime. Despite its relatively short duration, it is still an important chapter in baseball history.

Pitch Perfect

Baseball's Perfect Games

Another no-hitter for Sandy Koufax.

Perfect games are one of the rarest things in baseball. Only 23 perfect games have been thrown in baseball history, and each one has produced special memories. A perfect game is when a pitcher doesn't allow a single base runner to get on base, whether by hit, walk, or error, which is why the event is so rare. Considering that there have been over 300,000 games played in MLB history, the fact that there have been only 23 perfect games shows how magnificent a feat achieving one really is.

During the 19th century, two perfect games were thrown. The first was by Lee Richmond on June 12, 1880 for the Worcester Worcesters, and the second was thrown just five days later, on June 17, by John Montgomery Ward of the Providence Grays.

Twenty four years later, the first perfect game thrown in the World Series era was tossed by, appropriately enough, the great Cy Young, at the age of 37, in 1904 against the Philadelphia Athletics. The final score was 3-0, Boston Americans. It was one of the three no-hitters in Cy Young's illustrious career.

Another Hall of Famer, Addie Joss, tossed a perfect game on October 2, 1908 against the Cleveland Naps (Indians). The game lasted only an hour and 38 minutes, so obviously it was low scoring, 1-0 to be exact. Joss only threw 74 pitches during the game, which isn't that surprising, considering that he has the lowest WHIP and second lowest ERA in baseball history!! By the way, WHIP is a relatively new statistic which shows how many base runners a pitcher allows per inning. It is calculated by adding walks plus hits allowed and dividing by innings pitched. Joss's career WHIP was less than 1.00, a microscopic 0.9678. The average WHIP in MLB in 2013 was 1.3.

After Charlie Robertson tossed a perfecto for the White Sox in 1922, the perfect game came back after a 34-year break, and this time it came to the Fall Classic. In Game Five of the 1956 World Series, Don Larsen blanked the Dodgers, giving the Yankees a three games to two lead in the Series. Amazingly, to this day, Larsen's perfecto is the only no-hitter of any kind to have been pitched in the World Series. The image of catcher

Yogi Berra jumping into Larsen's arms is one of the most famous ever in baseball history.

After Hall of Famers Jim Bunning, Sandy Koufax and Catfish Hunter tossed perfectos and non-HoFers Len Barker, Mike Witt and Tom Browning did so as well in the three decades that followed, it was time for the first ever by a foreign-born player, Nicaraguan Dennis Martinez, who, while playing for the Montreal Expos in 1991, didn't allow a Dodger to get on base all game. Kenny Rogers was the next to achieve the feat, in a game for Texas in 1994 against the Angels, followed by two Yankees, David Wells in 1998, and then David Cone in 1999, whose was the first accomplished in interleague play. Randy Johnson threw the next perfecto in 2004 and, in the last six seasons alone, six other pitchers have joined the perfect game ranks—Mark Buehrle, Dallas Braden, Roy Halladay, Philip Humber, Matt Cain and finally Felix Hernandez.

Although these pitchers are the only ones to have thrown official perfect games, one other deserves mention, for what would have been the longest perfect game ever completed. His name is Harvey Haddix, who pitched 12 innings of perfect ball for the Pittsburgh Pirates against the Braves on May 26, 1959, but then lost it in the thirteenth on a walk, an error, and a walk-off double.

Well, the bottom line is, not everyone can be perfect. However, the ones who are, are a very special group of pitchers, a group that will never be forgotten.

Quality Quips

Famous Baseball Quotes

Yogi Berra is a New York Yankees Hall of Fame catcher who played from 1947-1963 and has the most World Series rings as a player of all time,

The incomparable Yogi Berra.

with ten. He hit a lot of balls out of the park, but is also very famous for speaking his own unique language. His statements had a certain logic to them, but in some ways made no sense whatsoever. For example, have you ever not wanted to go to a restaurant because "Nobody goes there anymore because it's too crowded?" Have you ever thought to yourself that you should "Always go to your friends' funerals, or else they won't come to yours?" Or while giving directions, told someone "When you come to the fork in the road, take it?" Well, if you haven't, then you are no Yogi Berra. But Yogi-isms go beyond funniness; some have become part of the great lore of the game. Imagine this: a team is down by seven runs in the late innings and comes back to win it. At the start of the rally Yogi probably would have said "It ain't over 'til it's over," one of the most famous quotes in baseball history, which Berra said to a reporter about halfway through the 1973 season when he was managing the Mets and, sure enough, the team made a huge second half comeback, and ended up winning the pennant.

There are countless other great baseball quotes. One of my favorites is "Hit 'em where they ain't," by Willie Keeler, another Hall of Famer. That's how he got so many hits – because he hit the ball where the fielders weren't. Of course, a lot of players got a lot of hits, but at this point the quote is so famous that Keeler is much better known for it than for his .341 lifetime batting average, nearly 3,000 career hits, and the fact that he struck out just 136 times in 8,591 career at bats.

Willie Stargell could also hit the ball well, but it was a lot harder for him than it looked. "They give you a round bat and they throw you a round ball and they tell you to hit it square." This quote may sound funny at first, but it really makes perfect sense. Hitting a baseball is very hard but, with enough practice, who knows, maybe you too can hit it just like the greats, the way Willie Stargell did.

Another great quote is one by Ty Cobb, which shows how confident he was in his hitting skills. When he was asked at age 73 how he would do against the modern day pitchers of the time he said he would only hit .300 because "You've got to remember – I'm seventy-three."

Announcers are often very wise with their words and have provided many great quotes over the years. A great example of this comes from Ernie Harwell, the legendary long-time broadcaster for the Tigers, who said in his 1955 article, "The Game for All America." "Baseball is a ballet without music. Drama without words." What a perfect way to describe America's national pastime! What Ernie meant was that baseball, like great art, provides fans with excitement, joy, sadness, and so many other emotions. Baseball is a way to grab the attention of family or friends and start a deep conversation that could last an eternity. Ernie was a huge fan of the game and this quote surely shows that.

Obviously, baseball writers are also known for their quotes, like this from Thomas Boswell: "More than any other American sport, baseball creates the magnetic, addictive illusion that it can almost be understood." It's true. Baseball is like a magnet that sticks to you your whole life and is addictive. But most of all, baseball is enjoyable on many different levels and fans are drawn to it (and love it) for many different reasons.

Rogers Hornsby was another great Hall of Famer with a great quote: "People ask me what I do in winter when there's no baseball. I'll tell you what I do. I stare out the window and wait for spring." That must be why he has the second highest career batting average among all the ballplayers in baseball history at .358. He was obsessed with the game that he loved.

One of the great things about baseball is that, at the end of the day, it's still a children's game. Hall of Famer Cal Ripken Jr. said it best when he said "you can be a kid for as long as you want when you play baseball." That sort of puts everything else into perspective.

Lou Gehrig is right up there with Cobb and Hornsby on the list of all-time greats. But the Iron Horse's career and life was cut short by an incurable disease called Amyotrophic Lateral Sclerosis. Gehrig made a speech at Yankee Stadium on July 4th, 1939, the last time he appeared in front of a Yankees crowd. In that speech, facing death, Gehrig said he considered himself "the luckiest man on the face of the earth." He then went on to say: "I might have had a tough break, but I have an awful lot to live for." With tears in their eyes, over 60,000 people in the stands stood and cheered for the great Gehrig. Sadly he would be gone just two years later. However, despite his untimely demise, Gehrig's play on the field and his farewell speech will never be forgotten.

So, quotes make baseball vibrant and fun, which is exactly what the game is meant to be.

Revolutionary Robinson

Jackie Robinson

One of the most revolutionary figures in baseball history was Babe Ruth. But there is someone much more revolutionary than even the Babe. This someone changed the game forever and integrated not just baseball, but other sports as well, and helped push forward the civil rights movement in the United States.

Jack (Jackie) Roosevelt Robinson was born on January 31, 1919, in Cairo, Georgia. Robinson's older brother, Matthew, inspired Jackie to pursue his talent and love for athletics. Matthew won a silver medal in the 200-meter dash, just behind Jesse Owens, at the 1936 Olympic Games in Berlin, Germany.

With Branch Rickey, on the eve of a baseball revolution.

Jackie turning two.

From 1942 to 1944, Jackie served as a second lieutenant in the United States Army. He never saw combat, but he was arrested and court-martialed when he refused to move to the back of a segregated bus during training. The courage that he showed then against racial segregation would ultimately be important for Robinson in Major League Baseball too.

After the Army, in 1944, Robinson began to play pro baseball, but because the sport was segregated (whites and blacks played in separate leagues), he began his career in the Negro Leagues. Jackie, though, was soon signed by Branch Rickey, general manager of the Brooklyn Dodgers, to help integrate Major League Baseball, and to help the Dodgers win. Robinson first joined the Montreal Royals, a Dodgers farm team, in 1946. Many people in the crowds jeered at Robinson, and he and his family received threats. Despite the challenges, Robinson excelled with the Royals, leading the International League in batting at .349. His excellent year led to his promotion to the major league Dodgers.

Jackie's debut game, on April 15, 1947, was the first time ever that an African-American athlete played in a Major League Baseball game. Truly a monumentally historic event!! The discrimination didn't stop, but there were those who defended Jackie, including Jewish baseball star and slugger Hank Greenberg and Dodgers shortstop and team captain Pee Wee Reese. One day, while fans harassed Robinson during a game, Reese walked over to him and put his arm around Jackie, a gesture that has become legendary in baseball history. The picture is even more iconic.

In his rookie year, Jackie hit 12 home runs, scored 125 runs, and helped the Dodgers win the pennant. That year, Robinson also led the league in stolen bases and was voted the Rookie of the Year. As his career went on, he continued to amaze everyone with his skills, including an outstanding .342 batting average during the 1949 season. That year, he earned his sole MVP Award.

Robinson soon became the highest-paid player in Dodgers history, and his success in the major leagues paved the way for other great African-American players to join the major leagues, such as teammates Roy Campanella and Don Newcombe, not to mention all-time greats like Willie Mays and Hank Aaron.

Ultimately, in his career with the Dodgers from 1947-1956, Robinson and his team won the National League pennant six times. Finally, after four World Series losses, in 1955, he helped the Dodgers win their only World Series in Brooklyn, an event that solidified Jackie's place in the Hall of Fame and in the hearts of baseball fans across the nation.

Today, in honor of Jackie Robinson's accomplishments, his number 42 is retired across all of Major League Baseball so that it will never be issued again. However, it is worn by every player in the major leagues on Jackie Robinson Day, April 15th, to further honor the great man.

Super Shots

Legendary Home Runs

"Stay fair!!"

Home runs are a very big part of baseball history. Most home runs are the result of a player hitting the ball over the fence, although sometimes the ball never even leaves the park (which is known as an inside the park home run). Some home runs are sort of expected, like when Frank Robinson hit another one out, and some are more of a surprise, like when Warren Spahn, a pitcher, went deep with one into the seats. Regardless, few things in baseball are more exciting than home runs, which is why people come to the ballpark to see the sluggers smack dingers into the bleachers.

So it is really not surprising that many of the greatest moments in baseball history are big home runs in big moments. That's the deal with some
of the "super shots" in baseball history.

Even though this homer has already been mentioned under "Booming
Babe," it deserves to be repeated, because it's the one and only "Called
Shot." Let's set the stage: Game Three of the 1932 World Series, Cubs vs.
Yankees. The game is tied at four when Babe Ruth comes to bat against
Charlie Root. The Chicago crowd is so loud that you can't hear the person
sitting next to you. Root throws two called strikes to Ruth. Ruth doesn't
like the calls, nor the merciless heckling, so he points his bat to center
field as if to say, "I'm gonna hit the next pitch right over that fence." And,
sure enough, he did! He smacked one of the longest homers ever hit at
Wrigley Field and the Yanks went on to win the Series in four straight.

No list of the greatest "super shots" in baseball history would be complete
without Henry Aaron's 715th career home run, passing the Babe on the all-
time home run list. This home run took place on April 8, 1974 in Atlanta-
Fulton County Stadium in Atlanta, Georgia in a game between the Atlanta
Braves and the Los Angeles Dodgers. In the bottom of the fourth inning,
Hank came up to the plate to face Dodger pitcher Al Downing and launched
number 715! The sellout crowd screamed with excitement as Henry Aaron
circled the bases, and the ovation went on for many minutes. Given the
drama and historical importance of the blast, there is no question it was
one of the greatest and most memorable home runs baseball has ever seen.

Another favorite homer, also very dramatic, took place in Game Six of the
1993 World Series, Blue Jays vs. Phillies, in Toronto. In the bottom of
the ninth the Phillies led 6-5, but there were two on and Joe Carter was
at the plate for the Jays. The Phillies pitcher was closer Mitch Williams,
nicknamed "Wild Thing." The count reached 2-2. Joe only needed a single to tie the game, but instead he drilled a liner down the left field line
that was a walk-off, World Series-winning homer! It was only the second
World Series-ending home run in history, and the only one that came
when the batting team was losing. The Pirates' Series-ending shocker by
Bill Mazeroski against the Yankees in 1960 (which Yankee fans still sob
about) came with the score tied.

A fairy tale ending for Joe Carter and the Jays.

Bucky Dent had a very famous homer in the 1978 one-game playoff to determine the winner of the AL East, the Yankees or the Red Sox, who were tied in the standings after 162 games. Dent, a light-hitting shortstop for New York, came up to bat in the top of the seventh inning at Fenway Park with two runners on and two out. The Yankees were down in the game, 2-0, and Dent's opportunity at the plate was one of the last chances the Yanks had to get back in the game. Dent shocked everyone by lofting a home run off Mike Torrez over the Green Monster, way out of the reach of Sox left fielder and Hall of Famer, Carl Yastrzemski. The Yanks took the lead and eventually won the game by a final score of 5-4. The Yankees went on to win the World Series against the Dodgers in six games, which would not have been possible without Bucky Dent's home run.

Three years earlier was another very exciting and miraculous home run at Fenway, this one off the bat of Carlton Fisk, a Hall of Fame catcher for the Red Sox. It came during Game Six of the 1975 World Series, with the Cincinnati Reds up on Boston in the Series, three games to two. This Fall Classic is considered one of the best of all time, each game having been more exciting than the previous. Game Six was far from an exception. It was the bottom of the twelfth inning and Fisk was leading off. The score was 6-6 and Pat Darcy was pitching for the Reds. Fisk, just like Dent, sent a long fly ball to left field. It

Maz touches third after launching his amazing World Series walk-off.

was curving towards the line, but the ball just made contact with the foul pole, meaning it was a home run! The Sox had tied the Series! Although they eventually lost Game Seven, the image of Carlton Fisk waving the ball fair, "causing" it to just stay inside the foul pole, is one of the most iconic in baseball history.

Finally, one of the greatest homers in history is Bobby Thomson's "Shot Heard Round the World." This came in 1951, when the New York Giants came back from a twelve-and-a-half-game deficit on August 13th to tie the Brooklyn Dodgers for the National League pennant. A three-game playoff was played to decide who would go to the World Series to face the Yankees. In the third and deciding game, the Giants entered the bottom of the ninth inning trailing 4-1. With the score 4-2 and two runners on, Bobby Thomson came to the plate against Ralph Branca and belted a line drive three-run home run into the left field bleachers! The famous call by announcer Russ Hodges, "The Giants win the pennant, the Giants win the pennant," repeated over and over, is legendary in itself. It was simple but true. The Giants had won the pennant, thanks to one of the most dramatic homers in baseball history.

Triumphant Trifectas

Triple Crown Winners

There are a number of rare feats in baseball history that are instantly historic, like perfect games and games that go 20 or more innings. One of the rarest statistical events in baseball is called a "Triple Crown." A player wins the Triple Crown when he leads the league in homers, RBIs and batting average. A Triple Crown is very rare because most players don't excel at both hitting for average and power. For example, an all-time great player, Philadelphia Phillies third baseman Mike Schmidt, led the league in homers eight times and RBIs four times, but never had an average above .290. Another great

The "Splendid Splinter" in full swing.

third baseman of the 1980s, George Brett, had over 3,000 hits in his career, and one year hit .390, but never hit over 30 dingers in a season. So, in order to win the Triple Crown, you have to be the best league's best overall hitter for the year. In fact, only 15 players have won it in the history of baseball, with just 14 winning it in the modern era (which started in 1900). That's probably why every retired Triple Crown winner from the modern era is in the Hall of Fame.

The only winner of the Triple Crown from the 1800's was Tip O'Neill in 1887 for the St. Louis Browns (who batted .435 with 14 HRs and 123 RBIs). Tip, though, is not in the Hall of Fame.

The first Triple Crown of the modern era was in 1901 and was accomplished by the great Napoleon Lajoie. That year for the Cleveland Indians he hit .426 with 14 homers and 125 RBIs. You're probably thinking: how in the world does someone lead the league with only 14 home runs? Well, it's simple: in the early years of baseball, the ball was not very lively, and players didn't aim for homers. The game was all about base hits and stolen bases. In other words, in the "Dead Ball Era" the name of the game was small ball, which explains why the next Triple Crown winner, the Tigers' Ty Cobb, needed only nine home runs in 1909 to go along with his .377 average and 107 RBI to win the Triple Crown.

After Babe Ruth made long balls famous, the homers really started to pile up, and Triple Crown winners become more common. In 1922 and 1925, Rogers Horsby won the NL Triple Crown, hitting 42 and 39 dingers, respectively, along with a batting average over .400 each time. After that, in 1933, Chuck Klein won the NL Triple Crown and Jimmie Foxx won the AL Triple Crown. This is the only time that two hitters won the Triple Crown in their respective leagues in the same year. After Hall of Famers Lou Gehrig, Joe Medwick and Ted Williams (twice) won the "Triumphant Trifecta," it was HoFer Mickey Mantle's turn. In 1956, the Commerce Comet hit .353 with 52 homers and 130 RBIs. If he had been healthier, he might have beaten Babe Ruth's single season home run record at the time of 60.

Next on the list came in 1966. After getting shipped away by the Reds for being "an old 30," Hall of Famer Frank Robinson won the AL Triple Crown playing for the Orioles, with a batting average of .316, 49 homers and 122 RBIs. Robinson won the AL MVP that year to go along with his 1961 NL MVP, making him the only player to win an MVP in each league. He also led his team to the AL pennant and a World Series triumph. Actually, a lot of players who have won the Triple Crown have led their teams to the Fall Classic. In total, seven teams with Triple Crown winners have won the pennant.

The last winner of the Triple Crown of the 20th century was Carl Yastrzemski who, in 1967 with the Red Sox, hit .326 with 44 homers and 121 RBIs. It was an "Impossible Dream" Season that year for the BoSox, who had finished ninth in a ten-team league the year before. More recently, in 2012, Miguel Cabrera of the Tigers won the Triple Crown, hitting .330 with 44 homers and 139 RBIs.

In total, in the modern MLB era, two players have won the Triple Crown twice, ten AL players have won it along with four NL players, and the longest span between two players winning the Triple Crown is 45 years. Only the greats have won the Triple Crown, and their "Triumphant Trifectas" are prime evidence of that greatness.

Tremendous Throwers

While the Triple Crown of baseball is usually understood to refer to hitting, there's also the lesser known pitching Triple Crown, which is accomplished when a pitcher leads his league in wins, strikeouts and ERA. Since 1900, the pitching Triple Crown has been won a total of 16 times in each league with multiple two-time winners, and three 3-time winners. The three-peaters are, not surprisingly, pitching legends Grover Cleveland Alexander, Walter Johnson and Sandy Koufax and, in Koufax's case, all his pitching Triple Crown totals led both leagues!!!

Grover Cleveland Alexander: Boy could this guy pitch!

Unbelievable Underdogs

Baseball's Greatest Upsets

"The Catch."

"Underdog" is not just a word used in baseball. It is a worldwide sports term used to describe a player or team that is expected to lose to a better-ranked opponent. Some of the greatest events in baseball history have involved underdogs and upsets, so here's a look at the cream of the crop.

The 1954 Indians are considered one of the greatest teams in baseball history. Led by Hall of Famers Al Rosen and Larry Doby at the plate and Early Wynn and Bob Feller on the mound, they won an incredible 111 games against just 43 losses, on their way to the World Series. The consensus was that the New York Giants were just lucky to be there and many people expected an Indians' sweep. What happened was exactly the opposite! The great Willie Mays shined in Game One, making his incredible over-the-shoulder catch to save two runs and shift the Series momentum to the Giants, which they rode to a shocking four-game sweep and the Say Hey Kid's one and only World Series ring.

Although some upsets are big news in baseball history, some are destined to be quickly overshadowed. For example, in the 2001 ALCS, the Yankees faced the 116-win Seattle Mariners with Rookie of the Year and AL MVP Ichiro Suzuki. However, the 95-win Yanks managed to win that series, but then got beaten in the World Series by the Arizona Diamondbacks, in the team's first-ever World Series appearance! Forget the Yanks beating a 116-win team, how do you think this Arizona team felt when it just dethroned the back-to-back-to-back World Series champions? Probably amazing! They were huge underdogs and became the fastest expansion team to win a World Series.

Three years later, the Yankees again made it to the American League Championship Series. This time, they faced their archrivals, the Boston Red Sox. The Red Sox were trying to win their first World Series since 1918, while the Yanks were trying to repeat as American League champions. Things worked out in the Yankees' favor for the first three games, putting them ahead three games to none. In fact, Game Three was won by New York by a final score of 19-8! But then something changed for the Red Sox. They won games four and five with walk-off hits in extra-inning thrillers, followed by a hard-fought 4-2 win in Game Six. By then, all the momentum was with the Sox and they completed their amazing comeback with a 10-3 blowout win. The Red Sox became the first team in baseball history to win a championship series after trailing three games to none. Boston then swept the Cardinals in the 2004 World Series, winning their first championship in 86 years, and ending the Curse of the Bambino once and for all. Now that is an underdog story for the ages.

Lastly, no baseball history upsets chapter would be complete without the 1969 Miracle Mets of New York. The Mets had never finished over .500 since their creation in 1962, yet they managed to beat one of the best teams of the '60s, the Baltimore Orioles, winners of 109 games that year, in the World Series. Going in, the Mets were probably the biggest underdogs ever in World Series history. Think about it like this: a grasshopper going up against boxing legend Muhammad Ali. And yet the Mets demolished them, taking four in a row after losing game one to earn the franchise's first title.

The "Amazin'" Mets.

That's the exciting thing about baseball. You never know what can happen when the teams take the field. A team that goes 162-0 can still lose to a team that goes 0-162. That's what makes the game so beautiful.

Vigorous Victors

The Winningest Pitchers of All Time

As this book runs out of chapters, it's time to write a bit more about some of the greatest and winningest pitchers ever to play the game.

Grover Cleveland Alexander

Grover Cleveland Alexander racked up 373 wins during a 20-year major league career with the Phillies, Cubs and Cardinals, tied for third most in Major League history. He led the league in ERA in five seasons, wins in six seasons, complete games in six seasons, and shutouts in seven. He won an amazing 28 games as a rookie in 1911. Alexander also won 30 or more games for three consecutive seasons, averaging more than 380 IP for those seasons, and, at age 39, pitched beautifully in relief in Game Seven of the 1926 World Series, after hurling a complete game win in Game Six.

Warren Spahn winds up.

Christy Mathewson

As popular as any player in the early 1900s, Christy Mathewson won 373 games over 17 seasons for the New York Giants while losing only 188! Using his famous fadeaway pitch (an early version of the screwball), Matty won at least 22 games for 12 straight years starting in 1903, winning 30 or more games four times. A veteran of four World Series, Mathewson's only title came in 1905 when he threw three shutouts against the A's, one of the great pitching feats in the history of Major League Baseball. He holds the modern National League mark with 37 wins in 1908. He is also one of the original five players elected into the Hall of Fame in 1936.

Warren Spahn

Spahn is the winningest left-hander in history with 363 victories, all but seven coming with the Braves. He was a 20-game winner 13 times, including six years in a row. He also led the National League in wins eight times. Spahn still holds the National League lifetime mark for innings pitched over his 21-year career, during which he hurled two no-hitters and won the 1957 Cy Young Award. He also served in the military from age 22-24. Had he not missed those years, he may well have won over 400 games in his career.

Pud Galvin

James "Pud" Galvin was baseball's first 300-game winner, playing in the 1870s and 1880s. The "Little Steam Engine" had a great pickoff move, but his pitching was even more masterful. Galvin pitched for 15 baseball seasons, winning 20 or more games ten times and twice topping the 40 win mark, something that has been done fewer than 20 times in all of history. When Galvin retired in 1892, he was the all-time career leader in wins, innings pitched, games started, complete games and shutouts.

Mariano Rivera

While not a starting pitcher, Mariano Rivera is considered the greatest closer in baseball history, and maybe even the greatest reliever. His accomplishments earned him a place on the Vigorous Victors list. A closer is a pitcher who comes in at the end of the game, usually in the eighth or ninth inning, to protect a lead. If the closer holds the lead and the game is not a blowout, he usually gets a save. Rivera has the most regular season saves of all time with 652. Even more amazing is that he saved a record 42 games in the post season, with an unbelievable ERA of 0.70 in 141 innings!! No wonder the Yankees won five World Series while he pitched for them.

Some other magnificent pitchers you might want to research include Kid Nichols, Mordecai Brown, Al Spalding, Ed Walsh, Rube Waddell, Jim Palmer, Whitey Ford, Bob Feller, Greg Maddux and Goose Gossage.

The "Sandman," Mariano Rivera, notches another save.

Wonderful World Series

A Recap of the Fall Classic

1927 World Series ticket.

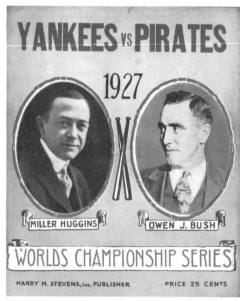

1927 World Series program.

A season of baseball competition boils down to October, when the best teams in the American and National Leagues go to the playoffs and compete for the World Series title. This makes the playoffs the most exciting time of the year. It doesn't matter how well the ten teams that currently make the postseason did in the regular season. All that really matters is how those teams perform in the playoffs when it all counts, and that by early November, one team is holding the World Series trophy.

The first World Series was held in 1903. It matched the Boston Americans (Red Sox) of the upstart American League against the Pittsburgh Pirates. With the help of Cy Young, Boston won the first ever World Series. It took until 1923 for the Yankees to win their first World Series, taking it in six games over the Giants. The '30s were ruled by the Cardinals and Yankees, with each team winning multiple titles in the decade.

The '40s were again dominated by the Cards and Yankees, but the '50s was all New York. At least one New York team appeared in nine of the ten World Series. And even the one World Series that wasn't New York-filled, 1959, featured the Dodgers against the White Sox, just two years removed from the Dodgers move from Brooklyn to LA.

After the Yankees dominated the early 1960's, an array of teams derailed their dynasty until the late '70s. In 1967, even the Red Sox got to a World Series, for the first time since 1946, although they lost four games to three to St. Louis, the same result as in '46.

The emergence of the A's highlighted the early 1970's, as they won back-to-back-to-back World Series from 1972-1974. Next, the Reds got into the mix, as the Big Red Machine

The three-peating A's of the early 1970s.

won consecutive Series in 1975 and 1976, followed by the Yankees who took the next two. It was in 1977 that Reggie Jackson earned the nickname of "Mr. October" for hitting three home runs in the Series-clinching Game Six. The '70s ended with the "We Are Family" Pirates winning the Series, their second of the decade, though this one was without the great Roberto Clemente, who died in a plane crash in 1972 at age 38, bringing relief supplies to earthquake victims in Nicaragua.

Parity was the name of the game in the 1980s, as nine different teams won the World Series. The Dodgers were the only team to take two titles, in strike-shortened 1981 and in 1988. The Phillies won their first World Series in the franchise's long history, and the Royals took their first as well, 16 years after joining the American League. The Brewers and Padres appeared in their first Series, though they both were defeated.

In the 1990's, the 1991 Twins won a classic Series against the Braves in the season of "worst to first," and then the Blue Jays won two in a row in 1992-1993. After losing twice, the Braves finally won their first Fall Classic in Atlanta. The Braves actually went to five World Series in the decade, losing two to the Yankees after their 1995 triumph. The Yankees finished the decade strong, winning the World Series in 1996, 1998, and 1999, after being shut out in the '80s.

1946 World Series ring.

Then the 2000's came along, and with them, the first championships for the Arizona Diamondbacks and the Angels, the second for the Marlins, the 27th for the Yankees, the tenth for the Cardinals (second most next to the Yanks), and the first for the Red Sox and White Sox since the 1910s.

In short, the World Series is the ultimate in baseball and, as such, has provided some of the greatest moments in history.

Exciting Extras

Amazing Extra Inning Games

Extra innings are an exciting part of baseball that gives it the feel of sudden death. The concept is simple: Extra innings are used to decide a winner of a game, if the game is tied after the ninth inning. Some games can take a long time, but sometimes they end quickly, like on a quick homer in the bottom of the tenth. Crazy things can happen in extra innings, things that may never be seen again.

On May 1, 1920, the Boston Braves and the Brooklyn Dodgers played to a 1-1 tie over a whopping 26 innings. That's almost three times the number of innings as in a regular game!! The game was called a draw, because back then there were no stadium lights to continue play once it got dark. (By the way, the first night game ever in the major leagues took place May 24, 1935, at Crosley Field in Ohio, in which the Reds hosted the Phillies.)

The longest game ever based on time was the 25 inning, eight hour, six minute marathon 7-6 victory by the White Sox over the Brewers on May 8, 1984. The game began at 7:30 PM, but after 17 innings was suspended until the next evening due to a curfew. The next night, each team scored three runs in the 21st to make the score 6-6. Finally, in the bottom of the 25th, Harold Baines of the White Sox homered to win it. Hall of Fame starting pitcher Tom Seaver won the game in relief.

The longest game in postseason history, whether measured by time or innings played, was Game Two of the 2014 National League Division

Baseball's Longest Game

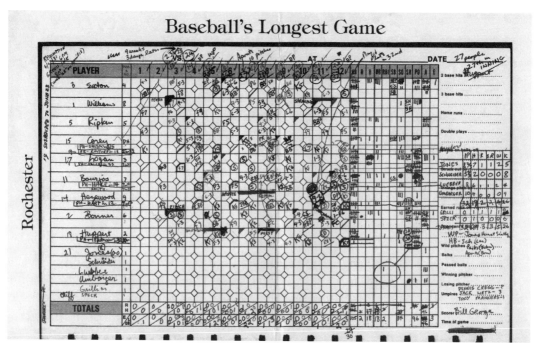

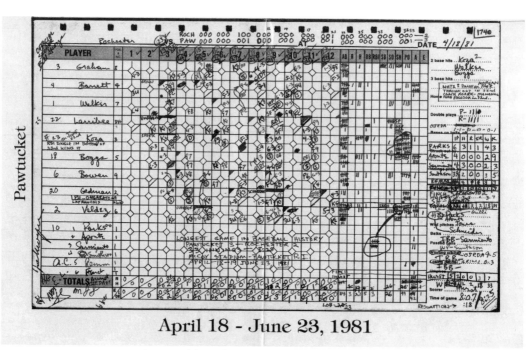

April 18 – June 23, 1981

Scorecard from the longest professional game ever.

Series between the San Franciso Giants and the Washington Nationals. The game, which took a record six hours and 23 minutes to finish, went on for a whopping 18 innings. The Nats were going to win the game but, in the top of the ninth, Giants third baseman Pablo (Kung Fu Panda) Sandoval doubled in the tying run. That run tied the game at 1-1 and it would stay that way until the 18th inning, when Giants first baseman Brandon Belt hit a solo homer, which gave the Giants a 2-1 lead, the score by which they won the game. San Francisco would go on to win that NLDS and eventually advanced to the 2014 World Series, where they faced and beat the Kansas City Royals in seven games, giving the team by the Bay their third championship in five years.

The second-longest postseason game (which lasted a mere five hours 50 minutes) was Game Four of the 2005 NLDS, Braves vs. Astros in Houston. Entering the bottom of the eighth, the Braves led 6-1. But the Astros mounted a comeback and, by the end of the bottom of the ninth, the game was tied at six. Once extra innings started, neither the Braves nor the Astros managed to score until the 18th inning. With one out and no men on base, Chris Burke of the Astros lifted a home run to left field. The home run won the game and the series for Houston and they would go on to win the franchise's first and only National League pennant.

While the previous games mentioned were long, they were short compared with the longest professional baseball game ever played. That game was actually a minor league game that began on April 18, 1981 between the Pawtucket Red Sox (featuring future Hall of Famer Wade Boggs) and the Rochester Red Wings (featuring future Hall of Famer Cal Ripken Jr.). The game lasted an unbelievable 33 innings and was finally won 3-2 by Pawtucket on June 23, 1981.

The moral of the story is try not to leave a game early, because you could miss an extra inning gem. And if you stay for a whole 20-inning game, consider yourself one of the sacred keepers of the history of the holy game of baseball.

Yeoman Young

Cy Young

While there are many great pitchers in baseball history, many of whom are mentioned in this book, there is a good reason why the best pitcher of the year in each league is awarded the Cy Young Award.

Denton True "Cy" Young was born in Gilmore, Ohio in 1867. He lived in a rural community and didn't get much of an education. He started playing in the major leagues in 1890 for the National League's Cleveland Spiders. In his debut he pitched a three-hit shutout, a definite sign of things to come. Young pitched 16 games in his rookie season and won a respectable nine of them. In his next two years, he won 27 and 36 games, respectively.

This guy won 511 games!

In 1901, when the American League was formed and became the second major league, the new league went after all the big stars from the National League, and the Boston Americans, commonly referred to today as the Red Sox, were able to sign Young to a big contract at the time ($3,500). Young proceeded to win 192 games for Boston in just eight years. He had an amazing year in 1901, winning 33 games with a miniscule 1.62 ERA (his lowest ever). It was the fourth of the five 30+ wins seasons of his career. In 1903, Cy helped his team get to the first ever World Series against the Pirates. He won two games and led the Americans to a win in the Series, five games to three. The next year, Cy pitched the first ever American League perfect game, one of his 26 wins on the season. In 1907 and 1908, although he was over 40 years old, he won 21 games in both seasons.

When Young finally retired in 1911, he had won an astronomical 511 games (an average of 23 wins per season with fifteen 20+ win seasons) and had a 2.63 ERA and 2,803 strikeouts. He was a true workhorse and still holds career records for games started, complete games, batters faced and innings pitched. Those numbers are definitely Hall of Fame-worthy, even though he also had the most losses in baseball history with 316. No matter, though. He didn't get an award named after him for nothing.

Youthful Yearning

While we're on the topic of "young" pitchers, the youngest to ever start a major league game is Jim Derrington, who at the age of 16 started the last game of the 1956 season for the Chicago White Sox. Derrington lasted six innings, and also holds the distinction of being the youngest player ever to record a base hit.

On the other side of the coin, the oldest person ever to pitch in an MLB game was the great Satchel Paige, who at the age of 59 pitched three innings for the Kansas City Athletics against the Boston Red Sox, and gave up just one hit (to HOFer Carl Yastrzemski), while striking out one.

Zero Zippers

A Brief History of Baseball Uniforms

As soon as you opened this book, you probably wondered, "What in the world is this guy going to write about for the letter Z?" Well, here goes. There is a vital item in baseball and in all other sports, and as you can see from the title, this item has no zippers. What is it? Easy: uniforms.

Jerseys, pants, hats and so much more have changed the way baseball players look since baseball became a commonly played sport. If you compare a ballplayer from the 21st century to a ballplayer from the 19th century, you would see they look totally different.

From the mid-1840s up until the 1870s, most baseball teams wore jerseys that looked like fireman's uniforms. In 1882, there was a rule that said that the uniform worn at each position on the diamond had to have a specific color scheme. This did not last long, as the colors were very confusing, but since then baseball teams all over the major leagues have experimented with different color schemes, especially over the last 40 years or so. Many teams wore powder blue uniforms during the 1970s and 1980s, including the Mariners, Brewers, Braves, Royals, and Angels. The Houston Astros wore rainbow-colored jerseys from 1975-1986. The Miami Marlins wore teal when they were first created in 1993. The San Diego Padres wore mustard yellow from 1969 into the early 1990s, and currently have an alternate uniform with a camouflage pattern, to honor their city's large military and naval bases. In an interesting move on July 27, 1999, the Mets changed their names to the "New York Mercury Mets" in honor of the "Turn Ahead The Clock" promotion sponsored by MLB

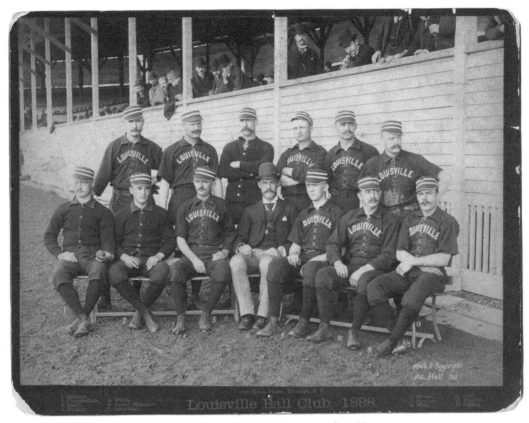

These uniforms don't look very comfortable.

in which teams wore futuristic uniforms. The Mercury Mets wore black uniforms featuring the ☿ symbol.

Numbers were not worn on uniforms on a regular basis until the late 1920s. The Cleveland Indians and the New York Yankees were the first teams to wear numbers on the backs of their uniforms. At that time, uniform numbers corresponded with the player's spot in the batting order, which is why Babe Ruth wore the number three and Lou Gehrig wore four. Both teams started this tradition in 1929 and it continues to this day, though the numbers now having nothing to do with the batting order. By the mid-1930s, every MLB team uniform had numbers on their home and away jerseys. Last names are also displayed on the backs of jerseys, except for the Yankees. Names were put on the backs of jerseys starting in the 1960s when TV viewers wanted to know who was who on the field without having to know the numbers of the players.

Early uniforms were not very comfortable to wear. From about 1870-1890, laced-front jerseys were commonly worn. Button-down jerseys became stylish after the turn of the century.

The first baseball jerseys were made out of just wool, and were very hot in the warm weather. Fortunately, technology has been incorporated over the years to make athletes more comfortable. By the 1960s, other lighter materials began to get used such as cotton, and then man-made products like nylon and dacron were introduced and are still used today.

Pullover jerseys have been used since the beginning of baseball, however their popularity has faded in the last 20 years as teams now use button-down fronts for their uniforms. At one time, zippered jerseys were the norm in baseball, from about the 1930s-1950s, but that fashion died in the 1980s, so now there are "zero zippers" in baseball.

Players (and their teams) are identified not just by the shirt that they wear, but also by the hat on their head. This is a critical part of an MLB player's uniform. Baseball hats have been around since the 1800s. At first, they were made of straw, but that proved to be not very durable. As soon as baseball hats began to be made of wool, the straw baseball hat disappeared. In 1901, the Detroit Tigers were the first team to add a logo to their hat, a tiger. The Pittsburgh Pirates had a unique tradition with their hats from 1976-1986. Hall of Famer Willie Stargell would give a player a "Stargell Star" when they contributed to the team in a positive manner. The stars would be stitched onto their hats. Obviously those stars helped the Pirates, as they won the 1979 World Series against the Baltimore Orioles while wearing the star-covered hats.

Besides Pittsburgh's stars, the Chicago White Sox had an interesting uniform twist during four games in August of 1976. Bill Veeck gained ownership of the team prior to the '76 season and said that he wanted to make the White Sox winners again. On August 8th (a doubleheader), 21st and 22nd, Chicago wore shorts in games. Sadly, making the Sox wear shorts didn't do them very much good. Although it was very comical to watch, the shorts made sliding hard for the players and they were very uncomfortable wearing them in general. The White Sox never wore shorts again and have been the only team to ever wear shorts during a game to this day.

Houston's 1970s rainbow-colored jerseys.

Hope that answers the question of "how in the world did you expect anyone to write about zippers in baseball?" The bottom line is, team uniforms have been part of baseball since the beginning and will continue to identify everyone's favorite team. So, what's your favorite uniform?

Baseball History Timeline

The Game's Greatest Moments at a Glance

June 19, 1846. The first game using the Cartwright rules is played.

April 22, 1876. The first ever National League game is played (the Boston Red Stockings beat the Philadelphia Athletics by a score of 6-5).

April 24, 1901. The first ever American League game is played (the Chicago White Stockings beat the Cleveland Blues by a score of 8-2).

October 1, 1903. The first ever World Series game is played (in the Series, the Boston Americans beat the Pittsburgh Pirates five games to three).

October 1, 1919. The first game of the 1919 World Series is played. In 1921, Commissioner Landis bans Shoeless Joe Jackson and seven of his Chicago White Sox teammates from baseball for life for throwing the 1919 World Series to the Cincinnati Reds.

January 3, 1920. Babe Ruth is sold to the Yankees from the Red Sox.

August 5, 1921. The first radio broadcast of a baseball game takes place.

October 15, 1923. The New York Yankees defeat the New York Giants to win their first World Series championship.

October 1, 1932. Babe Ruth's "called shot" takes place.

July 6, 1933. The first All Star game is played at Comiskey Park in Chicago.

May 24, 1935. The first MLB night game is played at Cincinnati's Crosley Field.

July 4, 1939. Lou Gehrig becomes the first player to have his number (4) retired by a team, the New York Yankees.

July 12, 1939. The Baseball Hall of Fame opens its doors in Cooperstown, NY.

July 17, 1941. Joe DiMaggio's 56-game hitting streak ends.

September 28, 1941. Ted Williams of the Boston Red Sox goes 6 for 8 in a season-ending doubleheader and raises his average to .406, the last player to bat over .400.

April 15, 1947. Jackie Robinson of the Brooklyn Dodgers breaks the color barrier.

October 3, 1951. Bobby Thomson of the New York Giants hits the "Shot Heard 'Round the World."

September 29, 1954. Willie Mays makes "The Catch."

October 8, 1956. Yankee pitcher Don Larsen hurls the only perfect game in World Series history (against the Brooklyn Dodgers).

April 18, 1958. The Dodgers play their first game in Los Angeles after leaving Brooklyn.

October 13, 1960. Bill Mazeroski hits a walk-off home run to win the World Series for the Pirates against the Yankees.

April 14, 1969. First MLB game is played on foreign soil as the Montreal Expos beat the St. Louis Cardinals 8-7.

December 31, 1972. Roberto Clemente of the Pittsburgh Pirates dies in an airplane crash while delivering earthquake relief aid to Nicaragua.

2 1982 02862 7861

April 6, 1973. Ron Blomberg of the New York Yankees becomes the first designated hitter ever.

April 8, 1974. Hank Aaron hits his 715th career home run, passing Babe Ruth for first place on the all-time list.

October 16, 1975. Carlton Fisk hits a walk-off home run for the Red Sox in Fenway Park in the bottom of the twelfth inning of Game Six of the 1975 World Series to tie the Series against the Reds at three games apiece.

September 8, 1985. Pete Rose passes Ty Cobb to become the all-time hits leader.

October 15, 1988. Kirk Gibson of the Dodgers hits a pinch hit home run in Game One of the World Series against the A's.

May 1, 1991. Rickey Henderson collects career stolen base 939, passing Lou Brock for the number one spot on the all-time list.

October 24, 1992. The Toronto Blue Jays are the first team from Canada to win the World Series.

October 23, 1993. Joe Carter of the Blue Jays hits a walk-off World Series-winning home run against the Phillies.

August 12, 1994. Baseball strike begins and the rest of the season (including the playoffs) is cancelled.

September 6, 1995. Cal Ripken Jr. of the Baltimore Orioles breaks Lou Gehrig's consecutive games streak.

June 12, 1997. The first regular season interleague game is played as the San Francisco Giants defeat the Texas Rangers 4-3.

October 27, 2004. The Boston Red Sox end the Curse of the Bambino and win the World Series ending an 86-year drought.